THE FLAT-TAX PRIMER

THE
FLAT-TAX
PRIMER

A Nonpartisan Guide to
What It Means for the Economy,
the Government—and You

Douglas R. Sease and Tom Herman
of *The Wall Street Journal*

VIKING

VIKING
Published by the Penguin Group
Penguin Books USA Inc., 375 Hudson Street, New York, New York 10014, U.S.A.
Penguin Books Ltd, 27 Wrights Lane, London W8 5TZ, England
Penguin Books Australia Ltd, Ringwood, Victoria, Australia
Penguin Books Canada Ltd, 10 Alcorn Avenue, Toronto, Ontario, Canada M4V 3B2
Penguin Books (N.Z.) Ltd, 182–190 Wairau Road, Auckland 10, New Zealand

Penguin Books Ltd, Registered Offices: Harmondsworth, Middlesex, England

First published in 1996 by Viking Penguin, a division of Penguin Books USA Inc.

1   3   5   7   9   10   8   6   4   2

Copyright © Douglas Sease and Tom Herman, 1996
All rights reserved

ISBN 0-670-87148-6
CIP data available

This book is printed on acid-free paper.

Printed in the United States of America
Set in Fairfield Light
Designed by Brian Mulligan

For Marilyn and Jane

ACKNOWLEDGMENTS

Our many thanks to those who helped this project come to fruition: Marion Maneker, our shepherd at Penguin; the experts at Deloitte & Touche in Washington, especially Clint Stretch, Randall D. Weiss, and Mark Garay; Barry Kramer, Deborah Lohse, and Cristina Lourosa, our colleagues at *The Wall Street Journal*, for their careful reading of the manuscript; and our wives, Marilyn Lytle Herman and Jane Sease, for putting up with us.

CONTENTS

INTRODUCTION

Is the U.S. income-tax system on the verge of momentous change? Only a decade after Washington approved some of the most significant tax-law changes in modern American history, intense debate is under way about proposals that would overhaul the basic way we tax ourselves. Put simply, a growing number of influential people, frustrated with the complexity of our tax system, want to scrap it, along with all its multiple rates, innumerable exclusions, exemptions, deductions, and forms and replace it with a simple one-rate system, a flat tax. If they prevail, it would be one of the most sweeping changes in U.S. history.

But is the current system so complex, so unfair, and so burdensome that it must be destroyed and replaced by something else? Many people say the answer is a resounding "yes!" It is difficult to underestimate the amount of anger, resentment, and confusion Americans feel about today's tax system. Critics point to the enormous amounts of time, energy, and money wasted by individuals and businesses in preparing their tax returns. They question the fairness of a system that in theory taxes people based on their ability to pay, yet grants many wealthy people enough loopholes that they wind up paying little or no taxes. They cite the competitive drag exerted by a tax code that first taxes corporate earnings and then taxes those earnings again when they are paid out as dividends. And they recognize the intense public concern that the current system allows—even encourages—far too much intrusion into our private lives by the Internal Revenue Service in its efforts to collect taxes. The answer, many say, is to abandon the current system and start from scratch. Doing so would lift an enormous dead weight from the economy and lead to significantly faster growth, improving our standard of living.

Flat-taxers clearly have struck a sensitive nerve. Nearly half of all U.S. taxpayers seek professional help to prepare their taxes. Granted, many seek help merely to avoid the aggravation and inconvenience of filling out tax forms. But others— many well-educated professionals and even tax experts—are so genuinely confounded by the complexity of their own returns that they strongly favor a thorough overhaul of the system. The tax code also has facets that discourage saving and investing, a clear paradox in a capitalist economy. And there isn't any question that of all U.S. government institutions, the IRS is the most feared and hated.

But in other respects, there is ample room for debate. Consider the question of "fairness." Who decides what is fair? Under the current tax code, one taxpayer's legitimate deduction is another's loophole. Who should be exempt from any taxes and who should bear the greatest burden? What is the purpose of our tax system? Is it merely to raise the revenue necessary to run the government? And how big should that government be? Or should we use taxes to influence economic and social change by encouraging investment in some areas, or by rewarding certain behavior? These are all questions worth arguing about. But they are also questions that we *have* been arguing about. For decades. The result of those arguments is our current tax system, the one that our elected representatives produced long ago and have been tinkering with ever since. While it is difficult to find many people who admire today's system, there are those who think that a system that is both simple and fair may be an impossibility.

Before taking a sledgehammer to the current system, it is also worth considering the risks of major changes. After all, even though this country hasn't enjoyed boom times in recent years, it has shown remarkable resiliency and long-term growth despite our cumbersome tax system. By any number of measures, the United States is the envy of the world's industrialized nations. From computer software to biotechnology to global finance, America sets the world standard in productivity and creativity. Countless new ventures are being started by entrepreneurs across the nation. Unemployment is relatively low, and inflation is tame. In short, we are hardly teetering on the brink of some economic abyss because of our system of taxation.

We all know rationally that taxes are absolutely necessary to the functioning of our government. Yet we resent the levels at which we are taxed, we feel inadequate in the face of the complexity of the tax system, and we fear the agency that administers that system. Politicians play on those resentments and fears to win or keep office and they are playing especially loudly these days. As a consequence, Americans can expect tax policy to be at the forefront of the political process for many years. The debate will often be rancorous, confusing, and emotional. Whatever change occurs will depend, in good measure, on how clearly voters and taxpayers understand what is being debated. We are writing this book to help you understand the debate.

As longtime observers of the world of taxes and finance—and even longer as taxpayers—we find some aspects of the flat-tax proposals highly appealing. Would you rather spend two weekends filling out the sixty-six-line Form 1040 along with Schedules A, B, and C, and Forms 2106, 4782, and 8829—or twenty minutes filling out a simple, one-page, ten-line form in which the most difficult math is multiplying one number by 17 percent? Yet as journalists we have watched over the years numerous misguided corporate and government financial schemes fail to meet their goals or crumble outright. So pardon us if we appear to be skeptical of the grander assertions made by flat-tax proponents who proclaim with certainty that their tax scheme will result in rapid economic growth and economic prosperity for all.

The truth is that *nobody* knows with any precision what would happen if this country tossed out its existing tax system and implemented something else. Our job, then, is to give you, the taxpayer, as straightforward an explanation as possible of the concept of the flat tax—what it is and isn't, what its proponents predict it will do, what its critics say it can't and shouldn't do, and what other alternatives are being discussed. In the end, you will have to make up your own mind.

We have tried to organize this book to make it as easy as possible to understand the scope of the flat-tax debate. In the first two chapters we give you what we hope is a mercifully brief history of how we got to the state of affairs we're in today. If you don't care how we got here, skip chapters 1 and 2.

Chapters 3 and 4 are the heart of the book, in which we explain the concept of the flat tax—including the perhaps startling revelation that it really *isn't* flat—and try to identify the ways in which it will affect you. We'll also show you some hypothetical cases of how the flat tax would affect the very wealthy, the very poor, and those in different family circumstances. But be warned, it isn't as simple as merely taking a fixed percentage of your wages and paying that to Uncle Sam. A flat tax could change much more than your tax rate. It could also cause fundamental changes in our economy, changes that no one can foresee. And some of the changes would affect you, for better or worse. You might, for instance, lose the ability to deduct your mortgage interest. Contributions to your favorite charity might no longer be deductible. Your employer would take a harder look at your benefits package.

Chapters 5 and 6 discuss how a flat tax would affect businesses. In chapter 7 we identify some of the key players in the tax debate, people and institutions you will want to listen to. It's important to know their biases and why they are in favor of or opposed to a flat tax. In the world of political reality, some sort of compromise is the most likely result of the tax debate. Chapter 8 is a discussion of some of those possible outcomes that fall short of the true believers' flat tax, but nevertheless address some of the problems with the current system.

We have tried to be as fair and balanced about the tax debate as possible. But there are lots of people on all sides of the issue who are smarter and have thought more about this than

xvi | INTRODUCTION

we have. Many of them have highly developed and clearly
articulated opinions about this subject. That's why in Chapter
9 we end the book with brief statements from well-known and
vocal proponents and opponents of the flat tax, as well as
other tax-overhaul proposals. Theirs are voices you should be
listening to, weighing their logic and philosophies against one
another before forming your own conclusion.

In the appendix you will find a question-and-answer discussion that tries to distill the tax debate down to its essence.
And finally, for those of you who find yourselves becoming tax
aficionados (don't laugh; we've seen it happen), there's a glos-
sary that attempts to leaven all this serious stuff with a little
tax humor.

Chapter One

A MERCIFULLY BRIEF HISTORY OF TAXES

From the dawn of civilization to the dawn of television sound bites and the Internet, people have been griping about taxes. Protests over taxes that were perceived as unfair or excessive have helped condemn more than one empire to history's scrap heap. Anti-tax fever, often evident in anti-tax wisecracks, dates back many centuries, as we are reminded by our friend Jeffery Yablon, a Washington tax lawyer. As a hobby, Yablon collects sayings about taxes, ranging from the old Jewish proverb "Taxes grow without rain" to a modern, anonymous, American quip: "There is untold wealth in America—especially at tax time."

The Yablon collection also includes some better-known observations, such as this one attributed to a seventeenth-century French statesman: "The art of taxation consists in so plucking the goose as to obtain the largest possible amount of feathers with the least possible amount of hissing." Or this one from former U.S. Senator Russell Long of Louisiana: "Don't tax you, don't tax me; tax the fellow behind the tree."

Flat-tax enthusiasts aren't sure who thought up the idea of the flat tax, or where it first may have been attempted. But this much is clear: However radical and revolutionary the idea may sound today, the flat-tax concept is anything but new. In its basic form, the idea resembles the ancient custom of "tithing," or handing over a flat 10 percent of whatever you make each year to some authority, be it the church, the local tax collector, or the monarch.

FLAT-TAX POPULIZERS

In more recent times, the work of several economists has greatly helped popularize the flat-tax concept. An important turning point came on March 25, 1981, when *The Wall Street Journal*'s editorial page published an article on the subject, "The Attraction of a Flat-Rate Tax System," by Alvin Rabushka, a senior fellow at the Hoover Institution at Stanford University. Rabushka recalls that he initially became fascinated with the flat-tax concept while doing research on the economy of Hong Kong, which comes fairly close to having a flat tax. After teaming up with a colleague, Robert E. Hall, a senior fellow at Hoover as well as a professor of economics at Stanford, the two set about developing the specifics of a flat-tax plan that was laid out on December 10, 1981, once again on the editorial page of *The Wall Street Journal*. That article provided the foundation for a large number of the flat-tax proposals that are in the headlines today.

Since their seminal *Wall Street Journal* article, Hall and Rabushka have continued to hone their idea, including proposals for handling the crucial transition to a flat tax from our current tax system. The result is a collection of three books— *Low Tax, Simple Tax, Flat Tax*, published in 1983, *The Flat*

Tax, published in 1985, and a second edition of that book published in 1995. Their writings have become the Bible of today's flat-tax movement. Senator Richard Shelby and House Majority Leader Dick Armey, both flat-tax enthusiasts, built their flat-tax legislative proposals around the core features of the Hall-Rabushka plan. The plan also was at the core of Steve Forbes's bid for the presidency. A longtime admirer, Forbes hosted a birthday party in 1995 in honor of Rabushka's fifty-fifth birthday at the elegant *Forbes* magazine offices in New York City. The centerpiece of the celebration: a flat cake.

Even with all its recent attention, the flat-tax concept certainly is not new to America. It has long been used in many states when setting sales taxes. The sales tax rate typically is the same whether you are Ross Perot or an unemployed steel worker. Medicare taxes also are imposed at a flat rate. What is new, of course, is today's attempt to impose a flat rate on income taxes.

TAXING AMERICA

Taxes long have played a prominent role in American history. Anti-tax fever led directly to the American Revolution and the rallying cry: "No taxation without representation!" That reminds us of another old saying: "Be careful what you wish for; you might get it." What would the Founding Fathers feel about the tax system we've produced today *with* representation?

The early debates in Congress over tax policy can provide lessons that we should keep in mind today, amid all the argument over how to tax ourselves. The question of what is a "fair" tax, for example, has been argued for much longer than you might suspect. In *The Federalist*, No. 36, Alexander

Hamilton wrote that taxes "shall be UNIFORM throughout the United States." (The capitalization is Hamilton's.) Yet Hamilton, in his later role as the nation's secretary of the Treasury, learned the hard way about the difficulty of defining what is "uniform." He reasoned that whiskey was a luxury and persuaded Congress to impose a uniform tax on whiskey. But while whiskey may have been a luxury in the saloons and homes of Boston, New York, and Philadelphia, it was something quite different on the western frontier (which was still at that point well east of the Mississippi). There whiskey was a form of currency. Farmers turned their corn and rye into whiskey so they could more easily carry it across the mountains and into the eastern seaboard cities, where it was traded for necessities. Thus the "uniform" tax on whiskey, while merely a nuisance to big-city barkeeps, became a threat to the well-being of the frontier citizenry. The resulting Whiskey Rebellion saw President George Washington calling out the militia and ended in the repeal of the hated tax. So much for imposing a "uniform" tax.

The income-tax system is such an integral part of our lives today that it may be tempting to assume it has always been a part of our history. The fact is that the income tax is a relative newcomer in America. The first national income tax came in the early 1860s, when the federal government needed help in financing the high cost of the Civil War. In 1862, Congress established the Bureau of Internal Revenue, with responsibility for collection of all internal taxes. It was renamed the Internal Revenue Service in 1953.

The income tax was not exactly popular. It lasted only about a decade. By the late 1800s, Washington generally was relying on tariffs and excise taxes to raise enough revenue to keep the federal government churning, inevitably leading to cries of unfairness from low-income Americans. Among the early champions of an income tax was William Jennings Bryan, the fiery orator who railed in Congress against the oppressive effects of tariffs and excise taxes.

"If taxation is a badge of freedom," he proclaimed, "let me assure my friend that the poor people of this country are covered all over with the insignia of freedom."

In 1894, Congress enacted an income tax, albeit a relatively modest one that hit only the very upper crust of American society. And it also proved very short-lived. In 1895, in the case of *Pollock v. Farmer's Loan and Trust Company*, the Supreme Court struck down the income tax. It said the tax was unconstitutional because it violated a provision prohibiting "direct" taxation without apportionment among the states.

The Supreme Court's 1895 decision killing the income tax only intensified the debate about who should pay and how much. That debate continued to rage until advocates, in 1913, accomplished the extraordinary feat of amending the U.S. Constitution to address the Supreme Court's problems with an income tax. The Sixteenth Amendment specifically gave Congress the power to collect taxes "on incomes from whatever source derived," without apportionment among the states.

Shortly after the amendment was passed, the income tax became the law of the land. But it applied only to the very wealthy. Only about 358,000 individual income-tax returns were filed for 1913, representing around 643,000 taxpayers, or less than 1 percent of the U.S. population. The top marginal rate was only 7 percent, and it applied to taxable incomes of more than $500,000. The average tax was only $78, or less than 1 percent of average "net income" at the time, an IRS publication reports.

SOCIAL ENGINEERS TAKE OVER

In passing the income tax, Congress made the crucial decision that the tax code would not only be a vehicle for raising funds to operate the government but also would be a tool to promote certain social and economic goals. That is very important to keep in mind when evaluating today's tax proposals. Many economists believe strongly that using the tax code for social engineering is a huge mistake, and that the tax laws should be merely for the purpose of raising revenue. But the urge to use the tax code to encourage or discourage behavior was—and still is—tremendously powerful among lawmakers.

Among the deductions allowed on that first return was "all interest paid within the year on personal indebtedness of taxpayer." Also generally deductible were national, state, county, school, and municipal taxes. Taxpayers could deduct losses suffered during the year that were incurred in "trade or arising from fires, storms, or shipwreck, and not compensated for by insurance or otherwise." They could also deduct bad debts and certain "reasonable" amounts for depreciation of business property. And they could deduct "the amount of necessary expenses actually paid in carrying on business, but not including business expenses of partnerships, and not including personal, living or family expenses."

The original Form 1040, issued in 1914 for 1913 returns, was only three pages long, plus a single page of instructions. Does that seem possible today, when even the simplest form, known as Form 1040EZ, has thirty-six pages of instructions? (There is no mystery as to how the dreaded Form 1040 got its name. The number 1040 was simply the next number up in the system of sequential numbering of forms developed by the Bureau of Internal Revenue).

Even in the early years, enforcement was a big headache. "It is clear that there were thousands of persons who failed altogether to make a return as required by law," the Treasury said. One explanation was "ignorance of the requirements of the law," according to a 1915 article. Sound familiar? Modern IRS agents hear that one every day.

But IRS statistics also show that enforcement then was more comprehensive than it is today. In recent years, the IRS typically has audited only about 1 or 2 percent of all the individual income-tax returns it receives. But the Bureau of Internal Revenue, as it was then known, audited 100 percent of the 358,000 returns for 1913.

COMPANIES ARE CAUGHT IN THE TAX NET

The first tax on corporate income preceded the personal income tax by four years. In 1909, the IRS levied a corporate income tax of 1 percent of "net income," and that applied only to corporations with net income over $5,000. There were 262,490 corporate returns filed for 1909.

Four years later came approval of the Sixteenth Amendment and the Revenue Act of 1913. Since then, the tax laws have imposed what a House Ways and Means Committee publication refers to as a "two-tiered" system of taxing corporate income. First, corporate earnings are taxed at the corporate level. Then, some of these earnings are generally taxed again when distributed as dividends to shareholders. This is often referred to as "double taxation," and it remains to this day one of the chief criticisms of U.S. tax laws.

The low personal income-tax rates that Americans went along with for 1913 didn't last long. Almost simultaneously with the outbreak of World War I, Congress began tinkering with the code, such as slashing the number of exemptions that had protected most Americans from the tax. The top marginal rate soared from 7 percent to an astounding 77 percent on incomes of $1 million or more. True, rates were reduced after the war, but never to anything close to their pre-war levels.

As the government's role in the economy expanded, the income-tax burden soared. The Depression, the New Deal and World War II led to an enormous surge in the number of Americans filing returns. In a thoughtful 1996 article in *Tax Notes*, a weekly publication, Joe Thorndike pointed out that the mass income tax was "less the product of careful planning than it was the child of necessity." By the early 1950s, the top rate had shot above 90 percent. During the early 1960s, President Kennedy—whose family deeply understood the impact of high marginal income tax rates—campaigned hard to slash the top rate. His words in 1962, cited recently by a tax commission headed by former Congressman Jack Kemp, still ring true among voters and tax-policy experts: ". . . it is a paradoxical truth that tax rates are too high today and tax revenues are too low, and the soundest way to raise the revenues in the long run is to cut the rates now."

Those stunningly high rates did come down, but Congress continued to cave in to increased efforts by special interest groups to gain relief from taxes. More and more special breaks were added, shrinking the base over which the income tax was spread, putting an increased burden on the remaining tax-payers who had not yet found relief. Some economists fought hard against the trend to shrink the tax base. But it was largely a losing battle. By the mid-1980s, the tax code was riddled with so many loopholes that the public began to demand major changes.

The flat tax enjoyed support early in the Reagan era. Ronald Reagan's conversion came during a golf game with George Shultz, then secretary of state, according to David Stockman, former head of the White House Office of Management and Budget. In his book about the Reagan years, Stockman says he doesn't know precisely when during the round that the subject came up, but that by the final hole, the president was convinced that a flat tax represented a way to cut the deficit without raising taxes. Eventually, however, top Treasury officials began to worry about the political implications of a flat tax that, among other things, eliminated the mortgage deduction, Stockman recalled. "So Shultz's original flat-tax idea was packed off to Siberia, in this case a 'deep study mode' at Treasury with a view to 'broadening, simplifying and reforming the income tax.'"

Reagan administration officials and many other tax specialists grew increasingly concerned about the large number of tax loopholes that had accumulated over the years. "Many of these tax preferences were enacted with the best of intentions," wrote Jeffrey H. Birnbaum and Alan S. Murray in their 1987 book, *Showdown at Gucci Gulch*. Those preferences "were supposed to provide 'incentives,' promoting laudable social or economic goals, but the sheer volume of the breaks became a menace. As the list expanded, the code became like a giant Swiss cheese with too many holes. It was on the verge of collapse."

The stage was set for the Tax Reform Act of 1986, a monumental effort to overhaul an ailing system—and the subject of the next chapter.

Chapter Two

Taxes Today

THE IMPOSSIBLE BECOMES THE INEVITABLE

It all seemed so extraordinarily implausible.

Even the experts in 1986 agreed that the idea of enacting a major tax-overhaul package seemed highly unlikely. How could Washington withstand intense lobbying from all those powerful special interests? How could skeptical voters be persuaded to plug long-cherished loopholes in exchange for lower rates? How could President Reagan find common ground with such Democratic leaders as House Ways and Means Committee Chairman Dan Rostenkowski?

Yet the historic tax act of 1986 was signed by President Reagan in October of that year, slashing the number of individual income-tax rates, jolting the tax-shelter business and raising corporate taxes. As *The Washington Post* put it: "The Impossible Became the Inevitable."

THIS IS PROGRESS?

Political leaders warmly congratulated themselves for this rare accomplishment. But since then, the number of tax rates—and the rates themselves—have been creeping back up again. It isn't surprising, then, that taxpayers today are more suspicious than ever of anyone who tries to convince them to give up yet more deductions in exchange for lower rates.

Today, the top rate is back above 40 percent, after including various cleverly disguised "backdoor" increases. Today, the code is bigger and fatter than ever. And today, many of the nation's leading tax experts say they wouldn't dream of doing their own tax returns because of the inordinate complexity.

Thus, it is not surprising that many people interpret the past ten years as a clear sign that the only solution is to eliminate the income-tax system entirely and replace it with something completely different. Even the much vaunted flat tax that this book is all about is vulnerable to the threat that future Congresses will simply take what starts as a low, single flat rate and raise it to the heavens.

Whatever the case, today's tax code is widely viewed with a mixture of disgust and horror. The closer experts get to our tax code, the worse it looks. Only a few years ago, suggestions that we scrap the current code would have been considered wild-eyed extremism. Today, such rhetoric is commonplace and apparently very welcome. House Ways and Means Committee Chairman Bill Archer, a Texas Republican, says voters "literally come unglued with excitement" when he tells them of his determination to get the IRS "completely out of our personal lives" and to "tear the income tax out by its roots and toss it overboard."

But it isn't just Republicans who are upset by the present

system. Here's House Minority Leader Richard Gephardt of Missouri: "We have so complicated the system, we've driven people crazy." And Senator Sam Nunn, the Georgia Democrat, calls the tax code "thousands of pages of pet rocks that have nothing to do with the national interest." Senator Nunn has joined with Senator Pete Domenici, a New Mexico Republican, in a plan that would overhaul the tax code.

Anger has been building for decades as tax complexity has mushroomed and as our tax burden has mounted. Today, the tax code resembles an attic where you have been storing all those lifelong possessions that you know you probably will never need but can't bear to part with. Now, that once-immaculate attic is a hopeless mishmash, piled high with mountains of old clothes, books, furniture, and other belongings. Nobody in your family can keep up with what is in there or find anything.

The evidence in favor of starting from scratch is large and growing. Consider:

❏ Nobody knows exactly what it costs to comply with the current income-tax system, but estimates range from about $75 billion to more than $300 billion a year.

❏ About half of all individual income-tax returns now are done by paid preparers, such as H&R Block, tax accountants, and lawyers. This figure has remained constant despite numerous Washington attempts to simplify the tax laws. Moreover, about 65 percent of all taxpayers who filed Form 1040 in 1994 paid someone else to figure out their return.

❏ Taxes now take by far the biggest single bite out of the average American worker's budget. Americans pay more in federal, state, and local taxes than they do for food, clothing, and housing combined, says the Tax Foundation, a nonprofit organization in Washington, D.C.

❑ In 1913, the entire federal tax law, plus explanations and other related material, fit into a single 400-page volume, says CCH Inc., a Riverwoods, Illinois-based publisher of tax information. As of late 1995, CCH's flagship publication totaled 40,500 pages in 22 volumes.

❑ In 1903, the IRS had only 400 employees. Working on commission, they collected $230 million in taxes, mostly from liquor, beer, tobacco, and margarine. Today, the IRS, with more than 114,000 employees, collects roughly $1.2 trillion, mostly from income and employment taxes. Its budget exceeds $7 billion.

Is this progress?

And it isn't just people who are hopping mad about tax-law complexity. Businesses are growing increasingly angry, too. At a House Ways and Means Committee hearing in 1995, Mobil Oil executives showed the company's 1993 federal income-tax return: nine thick volumes totaling 6,300 pages and weighing seventy-six pounds. William Dakin, Mobil's senior tax counsel, told the panel that it cost Mobil $10 million to prepare that return. And that, he said, was "just the tip of the iceberg." For example, work papers for Mobil's return totaled about 146,000 documents. That was up 27 percent from 1986, the year Congress passed a widely praised bill that was supposed to simplify the tax code.

The Internal Revenue Service: A Cruel Joke

To be fair, highly dedicated IRS officials are trying hard to simplify instructions and forms, as well as recordkeeping requirements. As we mentioned earlier, the IRS now audits only about 1 or 2 percent of all individual income-tax returns each year. And about 70 percent of all individual returns today take the standard deduction.

IRS officials also are trying harder to focus on customer service. IRS Commissioner Margaret Milner Richardson once optimistically said the agency has been recognized as "a leader among government agencies in customer service." But Commissioner Richardson's boast strikes some people as a joke. Humor columnist Dave Barry once said these words are comparable to stating that "cement is a leader among construction materials for use as a dessert topping."

IRS intrusiveness is a constant source of complaints. And taxpayer concern is likely to increase as more and more taxpayers are confronted by such IRS techniques as "economic reality," or "lifestyle," audits. In essence, these are audits in which IRS agents don't just look at what is within the four corners of your return. Instead, they examine your overall lifestyle—such as where you live, what kind of home you have, what kind of car you drive, and where you vacation—in an attempt to see if you are hiding taxable income. Even for those honest taxpayers who have reported every penny of income, these audits can be a time-consuming ordeal.

Taxpayers who are separated or divorced often face special woes. Under current law, anyone who signs a joint income-tax return may be potentially liable for all the taxes due on that return, even if the other spouse truly was to blame. In many cases, an accused husband or wife attempts to persuade the

IRS that he or she was an "innocent spouse." But under current law, that is very tough to do. Even if you can prove that you had no knowledge whatsoever that those back taxes were due, you will lose your case if you can't also prove that you didn't have any reason to know. In addition, there are several other obstacles you must overcome.

This issue can lead to huge problems when a marriage breaks up and the IRS later determines that the couple owes large amounts of back taxes. Current law allows the IRS to pursue either spouse, regardless of which one truly was responsible for running up the tab. Critics say the IRS all too often chases the spouse who is easiest to find and who has the most money. This problem has drawn so much attention that the IRS has launched a major study of it.

Despite all the tax-law changes in the past few decades, many of today's laws seem completely backward. For example, suppose you convince a court that you are right and the IRS was wrong. Now, you ask the court to make the IRS pay your legal fees, which can be considerable. It might seem logical to assume that the IRS should face the burden of proving that its claim was justified. Logical but wrong. Under current law, *you* must prove that the IRS was not "substantially justified" in bringing its case. Naturally, that is exceedingly tough to do.

That is part of the reason many people are reluctant to do battle with the IRS. Even if you win in court, you may lose because it's so hard to convince the court to make the IRS pay your legal fees. It's easier—and often less costly—just to cave in and pay whatever the IRS demands. Moreover, many people are so intimidated by the IRS and its enormous power that they readily fold whenever confronted by an IRS agent or even a confusing piece of correspondence.

A section of the Kemp Commission report on overhauling the tax code recounts the old story of the frog and hot water. If you drop a frog into a pot of boiling water, the frog will immediately hop out. But if you drop the frog into a pot of cool water and turn up the heat gradually, the frog won't notice the heat and eventually will boil to death.

"The American taxpayer is in hot water," the report concluded. "Escalating marginal tax rates, increasing complexity, and advancing intrusiveness have created a system that has reached the boiling point." It concluded that the current tax code "cannot be revised, should not be reinvented, and must not be retained."

But many tax specialists disagree strongly. They think the best solution lies not in a major overhaul but in tinkering. They also argue that today's code really isn't as complex as it may seem. For example, IRS Commissioner Richardson points out to flat-tax advocates that we already have essentially a flat tax for most taxpayers. She says 70 percent of individual taxpayers now pay at a 15 percent rate, which is also the lowest rate.

Critics, however, insist that we can do better. Some of the major ideas and their possible impact are outlined in coming chapters. When considering these ideas, it may be helpful to remember yet another old saying: The quest for perfection is often the enemy of the good.

Chapter Three

The Flat Tax: What It Is, What It Isn't

In its purest and most basic form, the concept of a flat tax is stunningly simple: Sweep away the present multitiered system and substitute a single rate. What would that rate be? Steve Forbes says 17 percent. Jack Kemp says somewhere south of 20 percent. Others say it would have to be significantly higher if we want to generate enough money to pay America's bills. Whatever the case, suffice it to say that the simplicity of a single rate is one of the main selling points cited by advocates of the flat tax.

But after that point, as we think you will see in the next four chapters, the flat-tax concept begins to get anything but simple. For starters, there are many ways to define what is taxable income. Let's also dispel a few popular myths about the flat tax. First, none of the most highly publicized flat-tax plans being peddled by politicians today really are flat. We will explain that little paradox shortly. Second, contrary to what you may be hearing from politicians and economists, it is virtually impossible for anyone to predict with precision how the flat tax will affect you or the nation. There is no shortage of educated guesses. But remember that they really are nothing more than guesses. Both the proponents and opponents of the flat-tax concept are making large numbers of assumptions about subjects that are inherently unpredictable. The honest ones will admit, when pressed, that there is no way to be absolutely certain about how things will work out on such hot-button issues as how much value your home would gain or lose if the mortgage deduction were eliminated, or whether your job security would increase or decrease.

There are many different flat-tax proposals floating around. To make an explanation of the concept of a flat tax as clear as possible, we are going to use as the basis for the discussion in this chapter the flat-tax proposal developed and honed over the last fifteen years by the two flat-tax gurus—Robert E. Hall and Alvin Rabushka—we met in chapter 1. These two, widely regarded as the intellectual fathers of the flat-tax plans floated by Steve Forbes and by House Majority Leader Dick Armey, have studied this subject intensely. Once we've explained how their flat-tax plans would work, we will discuss briefly how several of the other leading plans being advanced by various politicians would work. Then it's time for the opponents to have their say. We will show why some smart people think the flat-tax proposals are flawed ideas that sound great in theory but just won't work.

WHY A FLAT TAX?

There are several reasons that many people find a flat tax attractive. Simplicity is one of the big ones, although as we've already warned you, a flat tax isn't nearly as simple as it may look. One of the most appealing aspects of the plan advocated by Steve Forbes and others is that we could all file our income-tax returns on a postcard.

In developing their plan, Robert Hall and Alvin Rabushka were determined to attack the complexity of the current tax code. They have calculated (only economists would do this) that all the forms that the Internal Revenue Service sends out in a given year would stretch around the earth twenty-eight times. The paperwork costs our environment more than a quarter of a million trees.

Then there is the irritation of filling out each year's income tax return. For many of us, the minimum is a wasted weekend or two, or $60 paid to H&R Block or some other professional tax preparer. For those with complicated returns, the misery is compounded by uncertainty and fear. Even after consulting an expert, it is often impossible to know for sure if you have come up with the right numbers. There are so many gray areas of the tax code that if you ask a dozen experts for advice, you are likely to get twenty different replies. This won't strike many readers as news.

Twenty-five years ago, an Atlanta reporter for *The Wall Street Journal* asked five different tax-preparation services to figure out a friend's return. It was a fairly typical return—a family of four with all the usual deductions. But look what happened: At one extreme, a tax expert figured that the family was entitled to a refund of $652.04 from Washington. At the other extreme, another service calculated that the family *owed* Washington $141. That represents a difference of $793.04 (in much more valuable 1971 dollars) even though all the supposed experts were staring at the same set of figures.

But it isn't just professional tax preparers who get confused. The following year, *The Wall Street Journal* took another family's return to the IRS itself. The reporter submitted questions to IRS offices in five different cities: Atlanta, Des Moines, San Francisco, New York, and Rome, Georgia. Once again, the answers varied widely. At one extreme, Atlanta figured a refund of $177.14. But New York said $484.18. Many IRS officials couldn't even agree on how many forms the family should fill out. New York and San Francisco said four, but Des Moines said five, Atlanta said six, and Rome said seven.

Naturally, all this came before mountains of new tax laws, regulations, and court decisions of the late 1970s, 1980s and 1990s. Many of these laws were supposed to simplify the system. But when politicians start talking about tax simplification, it is usually a signal to buy stock in H&R Block and other professional preparers.

All the time and effort spent complying with the tax code represents a huge drain on the economy. Saving a large portion of that money is one of the aims of a flat tax.

Another goal of a simple tax code often cited by flat-tax advocates is to minimize the intrusiveness of the Internal Revenue Service, surely the most hated and feared of government agencies. The equation is pretty straightforward: the more complex the tax laws, the more effort the government has to expend to collect those taxes and defend against cheaters trying to take unfair or illegal advantage of the system. If we simplify the tax code, many areas of dispute and evasion that exist now will disappear. The IRS, which now has a vast army of more than 114,000 employees, could be shrunk. Indeed, some of the strongest advocates of eliminating the current tax system are former IRS officials who once had the unenviable responsibility of administering the mess we now call our tax code. Former IRS Commissioner Shirley Peterson says the current system is broken beyond repair, and that we need to start from scratch.

Fairness is another objective of the flat-taxers. The current federal income tax basically has five official rates ranging from 15 percent to 39.6 percent. But the actual top income-tax rate really is higher than 39.6 percent because of those sneaky "backdoor" increases that Washington stuck into the law several years ago. Among these are limits on personal exemptions and itemized deductions for upper-income taxpayers. Once your income exceeds a certain level, you begin to lose some of your itemized deductions and personal exemptions, effectively nudging that top rate higher. The top marginal rate for a married couple with two children would work out to more than 43 percent.

This system is supposed to be progressive—that is, to put the heaviest burden of financing the government on the shoulders of those most able to pay, while affording some relief to those least able to pay. But flat-taxers reply that there is a huge gulf between the way the system is supposed to work and the way it really does work. What is fair, they ask, about a system that purports to tax the wealthy at the highest rate, yet gives those same wealthy taxpayers large numbers of loopholes that allow them to slash or even eliminate their tax bill? Instead, they say, jettison the current system, simplify the definition of what is income, and substitute a single rate. At the same time, to make things even simpler, some people would also like to eliminate taxes on estates and gifts.

Loopholes aren't only for the wealthy. Even modestly paid workers can use such provisions as the deduction of mortgage interest to reduce their taxes. The mortgage-interest deduction was provided by Congress as an incentive for families to own their homes. But flat-tax advocates ask what is fair about two people, each with incomes of $50,000, who wind up paying sharply different tax bills because one owns a house and the other rents an apartment? In the end, of course, fairness is a philosophical concept, and you'll just have to decide for yourself what is and isn't fair.

The area in which you are likely to hear the most heated debate—and get the fewest certain answers—about the impact of a flat tax is the economy. Our economy is based on the risk and reward of private investment. It is private investment that creates the Microsofts and Wal-Marts as well as the local grocery store and shoe repair shop. It stands to reason, then, that we would want to encourage savings, which are put to work as investment capital building new factories and grocery stores and creating jobs.

But the current tax code is schizophrenic on that score. Some parts of the code are clearly intended to encourage savings. For example, the money you put in an Individual Retirement Account or that your company puts into your pension plan or 401(k) plan isn't taxed until you withdraw it years from now. Instead, the full amount sits in a long-term savings account or perhaps a mutual fund, available for use by growing businesses. But other parts of the tax code penalize investment. Let's assume that the company you work for earned a profit in 1995. The company pays taxes on that profit. If you own a few shares of your company's stock, you may be paid part of last year's profit—remember, that profit has already been taxed once—as a dividend. You'll have to pay taxes on those dividends. And if the stock price increases because the company has earned a lot of profits, you'll have to pay more taxes when you sell the stock. All those taxes paid on the same original earnings by your company can be enough to discourage people from saving.

The flat tax that Hall and Rabushka have formulated presumably would have several important effects. First, it would reduce overall taxes for many individuals, meaning that those people would keep more money for themselves. Because most of us work to get money, the flat-taxers assume that the possibility of being able to keep more of it would spur us to work harder, producing more goods and services more efficiently. The flat tax also would eliminate taxes on money that individuals earn from investments. That, presumably, would encourage people to save and invest the extra money left to them by their lower taxes. The availability of all that extra money being saved would help lead to lower interest rates. Voilà! With interest rates falling, everybody working harder and making more money to invest, the economy would grow, creating more jobs. The new workers would join their colleagues in paying their fair share of the income tax and government coffers would fill up. Pretty soon, the U.S. economy would begin accelerating at a faster clip.

But wait a minute. Have you noticed a flood of people eager to *leave* the United States to find a better life somewhere else? Isn't it just the opposite? If we opened the U.S. borders, wouldn't we be overwhelmed by a flood of immigrants seeking a better life *here?* The point is, the economy that we have created under the existing tax code is hardly some shabby Third World disaster. It is the world's preeminent economy, a vibrant, growing engine that generates millions of jobs and creates new industries. Could we do better? Probably. How much better? Nobody knows for sure. Opponents of the flat tax argue that while the current system could certainly go in for minor repairs and polishing, it isn't any-where near ready for the economic scrap heap.

They also contend that flat-taxers are wrong about what will happen to the average taxpayer's income under a flat tax. Instead of a tax cut, the opponents say, the average middle-income American will see an *increased* tax bill as much-used deductions disappear and they are forced to carry a larger share of the income-tax burden now shouldered by the rich.

DETAILS, DETAILS, DETAILS

We hope it is now obvious that this flat-tax stuff isn't as simple as you may have thought. What is on the surface a highly ap-pealing idea is really a very complex proposal to scrap a system that has served us well—perhaps not as well as we would like—and replace it with an entirely new and untested system whose impact is largely unpredictable. Let's spend some time now examining in closer detail the various components of the flat tax plan devised by Hall and Rabushka.

Their plan calls for a flat-tax rate of 19 percent on both in-dividuals and businesses. The reason that rate was chosen is very important. Basically, the two economists wanted a tax that would provide the government with approximately the same amount of revenue generated by the current system. Tax weenies call such a proposal "revenue neutral." A tax code that failed at least to match current revenues would result—absent any further big spending cuts by government—in a bigger budget deficit. That would certainly be running counter to the current sentiment in favor of reducing the deficit.

Hall and Rabushka also wanted the tax rate to be low enough to appeal to the vast majority of American taxpayers. They figured that 20 percent was a psychological barrier and it would be better to stay under that level. Let us note right now that there is considerable dispute about whether 19 percent would accomplish the goal of replacing the revenue generated by the existing tax code. The U.S. Treasury, for example, has done several studies and concluded that higher rates would be necessary, depending on how income is defined.

In any event, Hall and Rabushka calculated that to achieve a 19 percent tax rate, the nation's *tax base* would have to expand. We'll define the tax base as the total amount of income available to be taxed. Under the current system, huge amounts of personal income escape taxation. If the full amount had been available for taxation, we all could have been taxed at much lower rates than we were in 1992. And that's just the essence of what Hall and Rabushka want to do. To broaden the tax base sufficiently for a 19 percent rate to generate enough revenue, the Hall-Rabushka plan eliminates long-cherished deductions. That means no more mortgage interest deduction, no more deduction for state and local income or real-estate taxes, no exemptions for the elderly or blind, and no deductions for contributions to your church or favorite charities. These guys are tough!

But they aren't entirely heartless. They accept the notion that some people earn so little that they should be exempt from paying taxes. Thus, the Hall-Rabushka tax plan still permits certain exemptions: $16,500 for married couples filing jointly; $9,500 for single taxpayers; $14,000 for single heads of households (such as unmarried mothers); and $4,500 for each dependent. A family of four—father, mother, and two kids—would owe no taxes on the first $25,500 of income. And that's why the flat tax isn't really flat. Since everyone gets an exemption of some sort and pays 19 percent only on income above that level, the flat tax is mildly progressive. That is, people with big salaries will pay a higher tax rate than someone with a comfortable salary, and the person with the comfortable salary will pay proportionately more than a low-paid person. Here's a chart that illustrates the point. Note that if there were no exemptions, not only would the flat tax truly be flat, but it could also be set at a much lower rate and still be "revenue neutral."

THE NOT-SO-FLAT TAX

Percentage of Salary Paid as Income Tax Under the Hall-Rabushka Flat Tax for a Family of Four

Salary	Exemption	Amount Taxed at 19%	Tax Paid	Percent of Salary Paid in Taxes
$20,000	$25,500	—0—	—0—	—0—
$30,000	$25,500	$4,500	$855	3%
$50,000	$25,500	$24,500	$4,655	9%
$100,000	$25,500	$74,500	$14,155	14%
$250,000	$25,500	$224,500	$42,655	17%
$500,000	$25,500	$474,500	$90,155	18%

But with the exception of the exemption on that first chunk of income, there is little else a person can do to protect salary from taxes under the Hall-Rabushka flat tax. And with good reason. The more income that can be hidden from taxes, the higher the tax rate has to be on the remaining taxable income to generate the necessary revenue. Let's take a look now at some of the most common deductions and why flat-tax advo-cates are so determined to kill them off.

In 1992, according to Hall and Rabushka, itemized deduc-tions claimed on individual tax returns totaled more than $487 billion, a considerable sum of money. The largest category was that perennial favorite, home mortgage interest, which came to $194 billion. It was followed closely by deductions of state and local taxes totaling $159 billion, and contributions to charities came in a distant third at $63 billion. Altogether, those three accounted for $416 billion, or 85 percent of total deductions. Flat-tax advocates make a powerful argument that eliminating these deductions would certainly help broaden the tax base and contribute to a lower overall rate. Put the other way, if we continue to allow those deductions, everybody would have to pay a higher flat-tax rate to generate the same income now produced by the current tax code.

The flat-taxers also argue that there is a certain element of fairness in eliminating deductions. That's because under our current multitiered income tax system the same deduction will be more valuable to wealthy taxpayers than to poor tax-payers. We'll use the home mortgage interest deduction as an example. The wealthiest taxpayers—those who tend to own the most expensive houses and take out the biggest loans with which to buy them—get a tax break of more than 40 cents of every dollar they pay in mortgage interest up to a maximum of $1 million annually in interest payments on a regular mort-gage. Compare that to someone in only the 15 percent tax bracket. All he or she gets back from the IRS is 15 cents on each dollar of mortgage interest paid. The deduction is far more valuable to the wealthy taxpayer than the poor taxpayer, and the same is true of charitable contributions, which are claimed disproportionately by the wealthy.

We know, we know. You want to know what happens to the housing market and to your favorite charity if people can't claim deductions for mortgage interest and charitable giving. The only honest answer is: nobody knows for sure, and there are research reports on all sides of the issue. But we will explore some possibilities in the next chapter. Right now, let's continue to analyze the basic flat-tax proposal.

WHAT THE FLAT TAX DOESN'T TAX

As we've just seen, under a flat tax it would be well nigh impossible to shelter any but the exempt amounts of salary income from taxation. But there is a huge source of income that is now taxed that would be ENTIRELY EXEMPT from any personal income tax under the flat-tax proposals. We're talking about interest income, dividends, and capital gains on the sale of stocks, bonds, and other assets. To understand why Hall and Rabushka and other flat-tax advocates would knowingly surrender what probably looks to many of us like a grand way to spread the tax base even further—and thus get an even lower flat-tax rate—you have to think a minute about the way business is done in the United States. For the most part, private companies provide the goods and services that we purchase with our incomes. We tend to think of companies like General Electric, IBM, and Wal-Mart as *things* with an identity all their own. That's quite different from the way we think about our local shoe repair shop or ice cream parlor. They are more of a reflection of their owners, whom we often know personally. But the truth is, General Electric in some ways is just like the shoe repair store: it's owned by people just like us.

GE's owners are the hundreds of thousands of people who have bought GE shares. If GE does well, they do well, because GE pays them dividends and the price of GE's stock goes up. If GE does poorly, the shareholders suffer through reduced dividends and a lower share price. When GE earns a lot of money—we should say when the GE shareholders' company earns a lot of money—some of those profits are paid to the government in the form of corporate income taxes. Then—here's the important part—when the shareholders, through their representatives on GE's board, pay themselves a dividend from the leftover profits, they have to pay individual taxes on that amount. So the same dollar of profit is taxed first as corporate profits, then taxed again as a dividend payment. And if GE earns lots of profits (which are taxed), and its stock price rises as a result, the owners get taxed yet again when they sell those shares to someone else at a profit. Such "double taxation" isn't fair, argue flat-tax proponents.

What's more, they say, double taxation reduces the incentive you and every other American would otherwise have to own shares in GE or thousands of other companies. The amassing of money to buy such shares is called *capital formation*. It's how businesses get vital funding to start up and to grow in this country, and it is a critical element of our economic well being. Double taxation discourages capital formation and, as such, is seen by flat-tax advocates as a direct impediment to keeping our economy healthy. That, in a nutshell, is why advocates of this approach eliminate any taxes on income from dividends and capital gains. By making it more lucrative for individuals to own stocks, the flat tax is supposed to result in a more vibrant economy. In short, as President Kennedy once observed, a rising tide lifts all boats. Of course, since it's mostly wealthier people who own stocks and bonds, it isn't an accident that this portion of the flat tax would provide them with a bigger tax break than the little guy. We'll be discussing that point some more in the next chapter.

Double taxation also plays a role in the flat-tax advocates' treatment of interest earned on loans. Allowing companies to deduct the interest they pay on loans encourages those companies to borrow money instead of sell stock. Eliminate that incentive to borrow money, they argue, and companies will turn increasingly to the stock market to raise necessary funds. That sharply reduced demand for loans will result, they figure, in lower interest rates for everyone. And, as we will see a little further, lower interest rates are a crucial part of their argument in favor of a flat-tax system.

THE OTHER PART OF THE FLAT TAX—
THE BUSINESS TAX

We've just examined two major changes that the flat tax would make in the way most of us pay our taxes: some of our favorite deductions would disappear at the same time that taxes on some big sources of income—dividends, interest, and capital gains—would disappear. But we've only just touched on another big change in the making: business income taxes. Under the current system, corporations pay income taxes on their profits. Under a flat tax, they would continue to pay taxes, but flat-tax enthusiasts insist that the incredibly arcane and complicated system that now governs corporate taxes would disappear, just as the complex system of individual taxation would disappear. In its place would be a vastly simplified business tax that hits all businesses with a 19 percent flat tax rate, the same rate that individuals would pay. (See chapter 5 for details.) That rate isn't coincidental; remember that businesses are owned by people.

For companies like GE, the new system would be amazingly different from the current one. For example, the flat-tax proposal constructed by Hall and Rabushka would replace the current law's depreciation schedules with a simple provision allowing companies to write off the *entire cost* of new equipment in the year in which it was purchased.

Many of the costs of doing business would continue to be deductible. Basically, all a company would have to do is measure its gross revenues (the money it takes in selling its products or services), deduct its general business expenses (plant, equipment, travel, entertainment, etc.), and give the government a flat 19 percent of the difference. Like the individual tax return, the business return could be filed on a postcard.

But—here we go again—it isn't quite as simple as it looks. Consider that under the Hall-Rabushka plan, two big expenses at many companies—employee fringe benefits and interest expense on debt—wouldn't be deductible. We've already discussed why interest expenses wouldn't be deductible. Here's the thinking on fringe benefits: they are just another way to pay employees and, under the current tax system, a particularly attractive one. The company gets to deduct the expense, but the employee doesn't have to pay taxes on income received in the form of fringes. The government, obviously, misses out on some important revenue. The IRS could, of course, tax the fringes as income to the employee, but the value of the benefits is often difficult to calculate. If you simply don't allow the company to deduct the cost of the fringes, the tax is collected as part of the 19 percent business tax.

So what happens to fringe benefits like health insurance? That is unclear. Your company could still provide it, but clearly it would cost the company more. If you were running a big company, you might be tempted to reduce workers' salaries a bit to help pay for that added expense. Alternatively, the company could simply raise worker salaries and let the workers themselves pay for health insurance. We'll talk more about this in coming chapters.

What's the practical effect of this immense change in the way we tax businesses? It could be enormous. For example, businesses that borrow large amounts of money would be shocked by their tax bills if interest could no longer be deducted. But businesses with no debt that invested heavily in new plants and equipment would be helped enormously by the much faster write-offs of those new plants and equipment. But perhaps more to the point, businesses would pay a much larger share and individuals would pay a much smaller portion.

THE SEAMLESS TAX SYSTEM

We've discussed the major changes that would occur under the Hall-Rabushka flat-tax plan. They delve into much greater detail about those changes in their book, but that level of detail isn't necessary to grasp the essence of what they hope to accomplish. Simply put, it is this: an airtight tax system in which no income escapes taxation, but a system that results overall in lower taxes for the majority of Americans and a more productive and efficient economy. In effect, what they want to do is tax consumption and not tax savings. For our purposes, consumption essentially is the amount of money we spend on goods and services, and savings are whatever we have left at that point. A consumption tax—the Hall-Rabushka proposal is one of several ways a consumption tax could be imposed—is designed to tax only what is *taken out* of the economy, not what is *put in.*

Many people think it is important that a new tax system continue to produce about the same amount of revenue as the current one. Otherwise, unless the government slashed spending, the budget deficit would mushroom, forcing Washington to increase its borrowing, which in turn could push interest rates higher. As we have seen, under the Hall-Rabushka plan, businesses would pay a much larger share of the total taxes necessary for government to function. As far as fairness goes, Hall and Rabushka emphasize that because most business income goes to the rich, their plan would guarantee that the rich paid their fair share and that would allow lower taxes for working people.

GETTING THERE FROM HERE

Let's assume we all think the flat-tax system that we've just described is a winner. We all want a flat tax. Can we just decide one day that we're going to switch to the new system and abandon the old one?

Not a chance. Our current tax system has been around so long that all of us have made innumerable decisions about how we structure our lives based, at least in part, on taxes. Some of us own homes in large measure because we liked— and needed—the tax deduction on mortgage interest. Companies have bought equipment (or not bought it) and taken out loans based on the economic effects of our tax system. As with almost any complex and far-reaching change, there has to be some way to make a smooth transition from the old methods to the new.

Not surprisingly, the very thorough Hall and Rabushka have a plan to phase in changes to ease the strain. But even the most carefully thought-out transition-relief rules can lead to big problems. Remember that allowing transition relief means that the overall tax rate needs to be higher in order to avoid driving up the budget deficit. And if you set up transition rules for certain industries, such as housing and real estate, then how do you say no to hordes of other special-interest groups lobbying for similar relief? Writing transition rules can be highly complex, both economically and politically, according to Washington lawyers and former government officials who have been down this road.

THE REAL WORLD: TAX PLANS TO THINK ABOUT

To this point we've been discussing a flat-tax plan that is, in some ways, an idealistic plan. Hall and Rabushka aren't running for public office and they've had years to work out the details of their plan. In the real world—that is, the world in which people are trying to gain power by selling the American public on the idea of a flat tax, or some other change in the current tax system—things are a little different. Politicians must first get the attention of voters, then curry favor with them, addressing their hopes and fears—real or perceived—with ideas that will capture votes. Thus, it isn't surprising that advocates of big changes to our tax system are tailoring their plans to meet these challenges. The resulting plans vary—some a little, some a lot—from the flat-tax proposal that we've described, but all borrow big chunks of it. Let's take a look at several major plans for tax reform—both the flat tax and the not-so-flat tax—that have been floated lately.

THE FORBES FLAT TAX

If Hall and Rabushka have a frontline soldier for their plan, it's Steve Forbes, the wealthy publisher of *Forbes* magazine. Despite his professorial manner and monotone delivery, his message, trumpeted over the airwaves in multimillion-dollar advertising campaigns during his effort to win the Republican presidential nomination, attracted enormous enthusiasm. The Forbes flat-tax plan is modeled closely on the Hall-Rabushka plan, but he and his staff have made some key changes. Because of this tinkering, poor and low-income people come out significantly better under the Forbes plan than under the Hall-Rabushka plan.

The Forbes plan sounds tremendously appealing. "Start by scrapping the tax code," Mr. Forbes said in a speech in 1995. "Don't fiddle with it. Junk it. Throw it out. Bury it. Replace it with a pro-growth, pro-family tax cut that lowers tax rates to 17 percent across the board and expands exemptions for individuals and children so that a family of four would pay no taxes on the first $36,000 of income. Not one cent on the first $36,000. Anything over that would be taxed at a flat, fair 17 percent."

That sounds great to many voters not only because of its simplicity but also because it sounds like they will pay significantly less than they do now. To hammer home his message, Forbes frequently reminded listeners that his plan means no taxes on pensions, no taxes on Social Security, no taxes on personal savings, no taxes on capital gains—and no taxes on inheritances.

STEVE FORBES'S FLAT-TAX FORM

1. Wages & salary   1 _____

2. Taxpayer exemptions

   (a) $26,000 for married filing jointly

   (b) $13,000 for single

   (c) $17,000 for single head of household   2 _____

3. Number of dependents, not including spouse   3 _____

4. Deductions for dependents

   (line 3 multiplied by $5,000)   4 _____

5. Total deduction (line 2 plus line 4)   5 _____

6. Taxable income (subtract line 5 from line 1)   6 _____

7. Tax (17% of line 6)   7 _____

But at what cost? Either the government is going to have to cut back even more sharply on spending, or the federal budget deficit is going to get fatter faster. Slashing the budget would be fine with Mr. Forbes. He wants to eliminate "a whole alphabet soup" of federal agencies. But he also predicts that the lower taxes and lower interest rates that his plan would produce would stimulate a burst of economic activity that would generate more jobs and higher incomes for everyone. If that happened, he contends, his program eventually would produce enough revenue to close the budget gap. In that reasoning, Forbes sounds much like Ronald Reagan, who argued in the early 1980s that tax cuts would lead to more revenue, not less. But while tax rates were cut, government spending continued to surge at a breathtaking clip. The result: record budget deficits.

THE ARMEY-SHELBY FLAT TAX: VARIATIONS ON A THEME
This proposal comes from Senator Richard Shelby of Alabama and Representative Dick Armey, the House majority leader. Their plan, modeled after the Hall-Rabushka idea, has drawn warm praise from many frustrated taxpayers. A *Fortune* magazine cover story in 1995 called it the "most promising" of the radical reform plans. In a report rating the various tax-overhaul ideas, the Heritage Foundation in Washington gave this proposal an overall grade of "A," tying it for first place with the flat-tax plan of Steve Forbes. But the Treasury strongly dislikes it.

Senator Shelby and Representative Armey propose nothing less than repealing the entire Internal Revenue Code. In its place, their plan would adopt a single rate for individuals and businesses. For the first two years, the flat rate would be 20 percent; after that, it would fall to 17 percent.

Armey says the plan would raise only about $40 billion less than the current system does. He calls that "a modest tax cut" that would be paid for with spending cuts. He also predicts that his plan would slash the huge amount of tax-compliance costs, bolster economic growth, and lead to significantly lower interest rates. Under the plan, you could junk all those IRS forms and instructions. Your tax return would fit on a postcard.

Here is roughly what the postcard would look like for individuals:

ARMEY-SHELBY FLAT-TAX FORM
1998

1. Wages, salary and pensions   1 _____
2. Personal allowance
   - (a) $22,700 for married filing jointly
   - (b) $11,350 for single
   - (c) $14,850 for single head of household   2 _____
3. Number of dependents, not including spouse   3 _____
4. Personal allowances for dependents
   (line 3 multiplied by $5,300)   4 _____
5. Total personal allowances (line 2 plus line 4)   5 _____
6. Taxable wages
   (line 1 less line 5, if positive, otherwise zero)   6 _____
7. Tax (17% of line 6)   7 _____
8. Tax already paid   8 _____
9. Tax due (line 7 less line 8, if positive)   9 _____
10. Refund due (line 8 less line 7, if positive)   10 _____

"All too often, Americans are bogged down in a tax code that defies logic and serves only to hamper and frustrate the human spirit," says Senator Shelby. A flat tax, such as the Armey-Shelby plan, "removes the hurdles that frustrate entrepreneurs and unlocks the power of the individual." For more on the subject, see Senator Shelby's essay in chapter 9.

THE LUGAR NATIONAL RETAIL-SALES TAX

This plan beats even the flat tax for simplicity. It doesn't simplify the income tax, it gets rid of it. "We must make a decisive change in our tax system, not tinker at the edges," says Senator Richard Lugar, a Republican from Indiana. "I have concluded that the intrusive and complex income tax code should be abolished and replaced with a single-rate consumption tax on goods and services."

Senator Lugar's not-so-modest proposal would eliminate not only the income tax—both personal and corporate—but also capital-gains taxes and estate and gift taxes as well. This single-rate national sales tax would be administered by the states. It would exempt "necessities" of life in an effort to protect low-income people and the elderly from a disproportionate burden.

One big advantage is that more than 115 million people no longer would have to worry about filing income-tax returns each year. "There would be no records to keep or audits to fear," Senator Lugar said at a congressional hearing last year. "The money a person makes is his or her own. You don't have to report it. You don't have to hide it. You may decide if you want to save it, invest it or give it to your children. It is only when you buy something that you pay a tax. Although I applaud the efforts of flat-tax advocates to simplify tax forms, nothing could be more simple than no forms at all."

Besides citing simplicity, advocates also argue that this plan would help get at the huge underground economy. "When criminals and illegal aliens consume the proceeds of their activities, they will pay a tax," Senator Lugar says. Foreign tourists would help shoulder the expense of operating our government by paying the tax. Tax systems that rely on voluntary reporting of income "will never collect any of this revenue."

The basic concept of a national retail sales tax strongly appeals to other lawmakers, such as Representative Dan Schaefer, a Republican from Colorado, and Representative Billy Tauzin, a Republican from Louisiana.

THE VALUE-ADDED TAX

This idea is very popular outside the United States The "value added" part means the difference between the value of a business's sales and its purchases from other businesses, according to a handy guide to the tax debate prepared by the American Institute of Certified Public Accountants. Thus, a value-added tax (VAT) is "a tax on businesses that is collected as goods move through different stages of production." There are different types of VAT taxes, such as the credit-invoice method and the subtraction method. (VAT enthusiasts who want to dig more deeply into this murky field should get a copy of the AICPA publication, written by Martin A. Sullivan.) Suffice it to say that the subtraction method is widely considered to be simpler to use.

THE NUNN-DOMENICI USA TAX

We mentioned earlier that the Hall-Rabushka flat tax is a consumption tax. There's another type of consumption tax under discussion in Washington that you probably haven't heard as much about. Introduced as S. 722 by Senator Sam Nunn of Georgia and Senator Pete Domenici of New Mexico, it's called the "USA Tax Act." The USA in the title stands for Unlimited Savings Allowance and that pretty well describes what the 293-page bill is all about. This is *not* a flat tax by any stretch of the imagination. See Senator Domenici's essay in chapter 9. And unlike the flat-tax proposals that we've discussed, the USA Tax allows deductions for two of the most important items that are deductible under the current tax code: mortgage interest and charitable contributions. Additionally, it creates two new deductions, one for post-secondary education and training expenses and the other for net new savings.

If you think about it for a moment, this proposal has the

same fundamental aim as the flat-tax proposals we've already discussed: to encourage savings and investment. But it isn't a flat tax, and even some tax lawyers consider it complex.

THE ARCHER PLAN

Representative Bill Archer, the powerful chairman of the House Ways and Means Committee, wants to remove the Internal Revenue Service completely from the lives of the average individual. He wants to "tear the income tax out by its roots" and replace it with a broad-based consumption tax. We can't give you details because Representative Archer hasn't endorsed a specific plan yet. But he has laid out the general outlines in his essay in chapter 9.

Chairman Archer agrees that the flat tax certainly is better than the present system, but he feels we can do much better than that. As Senator Lugar has pointed out, the flat tax still requires you to file forms telling how much income you made, and it still requires a vast IRS apparatus to check up on everyone. That's why Chairman Archer wants to do away with the whole system and get the IRS out of people's lives completely.

THE CRITICS SPEAK

The easiest way to think about the issue of a flat tax for purposes of criticism is to divide it into two parts: the philosophical and the practical.

Let's address the philosophical first. Critics argue that the flat tax, far from changing just the mechanics of our tax system, changes its objectives as well. The income tax as we know it today not only raises funds for government, but also addresses questions of social and economic equality. We've already pointed out that the progressive rate structure is intended to put the heaviest tax burdens on those most able to bear them: the wealthy. The mortgage-interest deduction exists not to benefit the real-estate industry (although many homeowners fervently believe it does just that), but to encourage home ownership as something good for society. Owning a home, it is believed, contributes to the stability of the community because the owner has a stake in how well the community governs itself. The deduction for charitable contributions is aimed at providing an incentive to contribute to the well-being of those less fortunate or to the promotion of goals deemed worthy by the population at large, including education and the arts. It isn't an accident that the wealthy under the current system get the biggest breaks for making charitable contributions. They're the ones with money to give away.

Another objection is the simple question of risk. Leslie B. Samuels, the assistant secretary for tax policy in the Clinton Treasury, said the idea of replacing the income tax with a consumption tax would be "a grand experiment . . . that no other country has chosen to undertake. Proponents of these plans must, therefore, overcome a significant hurdle—they must show that it is worthwhile to conduct this experiment on the world's largest and most complex economy."

To clear such a hurdle, the flat-taxers must demonstrate convincingly that their plans would solve some practical problems, not the least of which is bringing the federal budget deficit under control. The Treasury Department contends that not even the higher tax rate of the original Hall-Rabushka flat-tax plan would accomplish that goal. And when flat-taxers argue that the lower rates and taxes they envision would generate enough additional economic growth to supply the needed tax revenue to balance the budget, critics cite statistics—including the bulging deficits from Ronald Reagan's administration—that they say call that theory into question. In short, opponents say, the flat-tax proposals now on the table can't clear the hurdle. Some critics also charge that the flat-tax plan would be bad for the economy because it would increase the overall tax burden on business.

Even some people who are attracted to the idea of a single low flat-tax rate are worried about embracing the concept. They fear giving away many of their long-cherished deductions today in exchange for a low-sounding flat-tax rate might be a bad bargain because revenue-hungry Washingtonians might raise that rate sharply in future years. Let those who dispute this argument remember what happened in the decade after the 1986 tax act.

Then there are critics who say that no matter what tax system you come up with, there will inevitably be enormous complexity as people try to wriggle out of paying. For example, even under the seemingly simple flat tax, businesses would have a powerful incentive to restructure transactions to cut their tax bill. Several skilled tax lawyers already are hard at work figuring out how that could be done. They insist it would not be difficult.

Moreover, the flat-tax system still would leave many dense questions hanging. For example, there would still be intense controversy over what happens when a married couple breaks up and the IRS later claims the couple owed back taxes. Who should pay those taxes? That's why some people advocate eliminating joint filing and forcing everyone to file separately. This question would, however, be handled very neatly by the Lugar approach of a national sales tax.

But Senator Lugar's sales-tax plan has drawn heavy criticism on several fronts. First, national sales taxes have a bad name among many economists—and politicians—because they hit hardest at those least able to pay: the poor. The poor generally spend a much larger proportion of their income buying necessities than the wealthy do. There are ways around that problem, of course, such as exempting such necessities as food, health care, and clothing, or providing rebates to taxpayers below some threshold level of earnings. Another key question revolves around enforcement. Skeptics say it would be very tough for even the best tax collectors to patrol all the tiny retail establishments across America and make sure a national sales tax was being collected—and that enforcement was being done on a uniform basis nationally.

That's why some people prefer the value-added tax approach, where the tax is collected at multiple stages. But critics fear a VAT would be very costly and burdensome to administer.

Whatever system you choose, though, don't expect the IRS to disappear anytime soon. Unless human nature changes drastically, it's clear that there will always need to be some powerful federal agency assigned to collect the taxes and police the system. And that agency will never win any popularity contests.

All in all, some people think the best answer is to resist the temptation to tear up the entire system and start from scratch. Instead, they recommend tinkering with today's system in an attempt to make it simpler and fairer. We'll examine some possible outcomes of such an approach in later chapters. But now it's time to look at who wins and who loses under a flat-tax system. And you'll be able to figure out how you might fare.

Chapter Four

Who Wins?
Who Loses?

After generations of tinkering, Washington has constructed a complex machine that only a tax lawyer could love. But tearing up that machine and replacing it with a simple flat tax, appealing as that may seem, would lead to big changes in American life. Few people agree on just what those changes would be, but speculating about them has generated a whole new industry: instant analysis of who wins and who loses under the various tax plans being floated. Even if the flat-tax concept falls flat and eventually is swept into history's dustbin, it will have made a significant contribution to American economic growth in 1995 and 1996. That's obvious in the mounds of flat-tax analyses, both pro and con, that have buried our desks in recent months. Somebody was paid to produce all those words and numbers.

What is most remarkable about all these weighty tomes isn't the razor-sharp analysis or the impressive number-crunching. Rather, it is amazing that so many smart people can reach such drastically different conclusions looking at the same data. Flat-tax enthusiasts insist their idea would lead to the best of all possible worlds—a much simpler, fairer system that generates more jobs, higher incomes, and, overall, a much healthier economy for us and our children. Nonsense, critics reply. Some counter that flat-tax plans would be "budget busters," leaving us in even deeper hock than we are already. They insist that either the flat-tax rate would have to rise sharply, thus torpedoing the popularity of the idea, or government spending must fall, forcing further painful cutbacks in programs that many people don't want to see disappear. Critics also contend that the middle class typically would wind up paying more, while the rich would get a big break.

Advocates and critics clash on many other issues, among them: What would happen to real-estate prices if Congress eliminates the mortgage-interest deduction? Will charities be placed on the endangered-species list if Congress wipes out the deduction for donations? What types of families would pay more, and who would pay less?

After plowing through numerous volumes and attending conferences on these and related issues, we saw clearly that it is not as simple to figure out who wins and who loses as advocates or critics would have you believe. Anyone looking for unequivocal answers will be disappointed. For the moment, this is an area filled with far more questions than answers. Yet it is still worth examining these issues because it is difficult to underestimate the remarkable impact of tax-law changes on our economy and on our daily lives.

In this chapter, we will show you, with the help of expert number-crunchers at the accounting firm of Deloitte & Touche, how a flat-tax system would affect a wide variety of people with different incomes and economic circumstances.

We suggest you pull out your latest income-tax return and use the information on it to calculate your own gains or losses under a flat tax. But even if you come out way ahead under the flat-tax plan, don't think that's all there is to deciding if you want a flat tax. For example, ask yourself if, to get the benefits of a flat tax, you would be willing to see the value of your house drop 10 percent? How about 20 percent? Would you be willing to see your favorite charity disappear? How much are you willing to pay for all those fringe benefits you get at work? The flat-taxers assure us that none of these will really be a problem under a flat tax. But ask yourself this: What if they're wrong?

After all, flat-taxers would lead us into largely uncharted waters. This would be an extraordinary experiment with the world's biggest and richest economy. Flat-tax advocates argue that we should try their idea anyway because our current tax code weighs heavily on hardworking citizens and businesses, keeping economic growth well below what it could and should be. But others fear the cure might be worse than the disease. Even if the flat-tax advocates are right about some things, the consequences still are hard to predict.

Among the biggest questions is what would happen to interest rates. Flat-taxers say rates would go down—significantly. But would they? Other economists aren't so sure. First of all, if we have learned anything from the past few decades, surely we have learned how hard it is to predict interest-rate movements. Moreover, we have learned that tax policy is only one of many influences on interest rates. Indeed, many economists would say that tax policy certainly is not the most important influence. Instead, they focus on the Federal Reserve System, which controls the growth of the nation's money supply. They also focus on long-term trends in inflation as well as other major industrialized nations' monetary policies. See what we mean about this not being so simple?

Even with all the question marks about what might happen if we went to a flat-tax system, there clearly is at least one way in which we would all be winners: filling out our tax returns would be much easier. For the sake of argument—and to impress you with the potential savings—we are using the 17 percent rate advocated by Representative Dick Armey in his original flat-tax proposal, rather than the 19 percent rate that Messrs. Hall and Rabushka have suggested is necessary. (Keep in mind, though, that a revised version of the Armey-Shelby plan would start at 20 percent for the first two years and change to 17 percent in later years.) But we're also calculating taxes based on a 20.8 percent flat-tax rate that the Treasury Department contends would be necessary. And at the end of the chapter we'll tell you more about why the Treasury reaches the conclusion that for the vast majority of workers making less than $200,000 a year, the flat tax will actually result in *higher* overall tax bills. Your tax bill under this or any other flat-tax system will depend on such factors as the rate, the standard exemption, the mix of your income between salary and investments, and the number of dependents in your family.

While it is difficult to make many generalizations about the impact of flat-tax plans such as those proposed by Steve Forbes, Representative Armey, and Senator Shelby, there is widespread agreement on at least these issues:

❑ Among the biggest winners would be heirs and heiresses to large fortunes. The reason is simple: several flat-tax plans would completely eliminate estate and gift taxes. Gone would be the need for costly estate-planning consultations and complex trusts. Senator Lugar's single-rate retail-sales tax also would sweep away estate and gift taxes. This is an extraordinarily important and sensitive issue to many baby boomers. For example, the tax on an estate of $3 million would be about $1 million. Critics reply that eliminating these taxes would be an unfair giveaway to a relatively small number of very wealthy people.

❑ Elimination of gift and estate taxes would be bad news for the armies of estate-tax lawyers, accountants, tax preparers, and other advisers in this highly complex field.

❑ A simple flat-tax system probably would be bad news for investors who own stock in H&R Block or other tax preparers.

❑ Many charities would almost certainly be hurt. Donors would no longer be able to deduct gifts and the charity itself would no longer be tax exempt. Charities today are big business in America. How much they would be affected, though, is anyone's guess. We will discuss that in further detail in chapter 6.

❑ Investors holding tax-exempt municipal bonds probably would be hurt badly by any tax plan that eliminates taxes on all investment income, including interest. There would no longer be an incentive for investors to search for tax-exempt income in the municipal-bond market. This is no small worry. The Public Securities Association, a New York–based trade group, estimates that the market for state and local government bonds now totals more than $1.2 trillion.

❑ State and local governments might see their own costs of borrowing rise at the same time that the elimination of the deduction for state and local tax payments puts pressure on local governments to slash taxes and spending.

The rest of this chapter is devoted to exploring how a flat tax would affect various people in various income categories, ranging from very rich to very poor. But as you look at the answers, keep in mind that there are many other issues, especially the key question of how the overall economy might respond to a flat tax. Again, the advocates make it sound as though everyone would gain. *But what if they're wrong?*

Randall D. Weiss, director of tax economics at Deloitte & Touche in Washington, urges readers to keep in mind two important points before drawing conclusions from the following examples. First, these examples show people with average levels of itemized deductions. Many people will have considerably more deductions than these, and thus they may be much more adversely affected by repeal of the deductions than the people in the examples. For instance, residents of high-tax states such as New York would be more affected by the loss of state and local tax deductions than residents of other states. Second, all the examples assume no change in people's incomes in the event that a flat-tax plan is enacted. "Undoubtedly," says Mr. Weiss, "there will be some changes."

Whatever the case, at this point we still think it is useful as a first approximation to give you a few examples from Deloitte & Touche without making any assumptions about how the economy might change in a flat-tax era. These examples are for 1996.

The Rich Get Richer

Let's start with the certain winners of a flat tax: the rich. Make no mistake about it, almost all wealthy people would get a significant break from a switch to any of the most widely discussed flat-tax systems. There are two reasons for that. First, under major flat-tax proposals, investment income—interest payments, dividends, and capital gains—wouldn't be taxed at all. Obviously, rich people collect more investment income than any other group in America. So that investment income wouldn't be taxed under a flat-tax system. Consider what that might mean to the really fabulously wealthy. The flat tax would mean that they could fire all those lawyers and accountants (saving thousands of dollars right there), still have an income of literally millions of dollars, and owe *zero income tax.*

Second, rich people who work for a living, such as the senior executives of big companies or investment bankers on Wall Street, would see their tax rate plunge. Instead of being confronted by a top marginal rate on their pay of more than 40 percent, they would be faced with a flat-tax rate far below that. In Example 1, let's look at what that would mean for a hypothetical executive with a wife and two children and an annual income of $1,000,000. We'll say most of it—$740,000—comes from salary and the remainder is split between capital gains of, say, $160,000 and interest and dividends of $100,000. And our executive pays $40,000 in mortgage interest, donates $30,000 to charity, and takes other deductions totaling $60,000.

EXAMPLE 1

$1 Million Income

Married Taxpayers

Total Income	$1,000,000
Wages	$ 740,000
Capital Gains (Losses)	$ 160,000
Interest & Dividends	$ 100,000
Home Mortgage Interest Paid	$ 40,000
Charitable Contributions	$ 30,000
Other Itemized Deductions	$ 60,000
Number of Children	2

	Tax under current law	A revenue-neutral flat tax at 20.8%	Tax under Armey-Shelby-type flat tax at 17%
Net tax liability	$311,439	$147,389	$120,462
Increase or decrease from present law		−$164,050	−$190,977
% increase or decrease from present law		−53%	−61%

Not bad, that $190,977 savings. That's a tax cut of more than 61 percent! Even under a flat-tax system set at 20.8 percent, the rate the Treasury Department figures would be necessary for a flat-tax system to equal the revenue produced under the current tax code, the savings would be $164,050, a 53 percent tax cut.

Creating Jobs and Businesses

Flat-tax advocates make much ado about how their system would encourage entrepreneurs to start new companies. And

it's true that our current system can make it a little difficult
and expensive to launch a new business—but not so expensive or difficult, however, as to stop Bill Gates from starting
Microsoft, or to stop hundreds of thousands of other entrepreneurs from starting their own businesses, whether they be cof-
fee shops or manufacturing companies or accounting firms.
We don't know how much in income taxes Bill Gates has paid
over the years as he has sold off portions of his Microsoft
stock. But we do know what he would owe on those stock
sales under the flat tax: zero.

THE MERELY AFFLUENT

Let's leave the rarefied heights of the rich and look for a moment at the ranks of the merely affluent. In Example 2, let's
assume a vice president at a big company earns an annual
base salary of $300,000. Because he has done well and his
company earned a lot of money last year, we'll give him a
$50,000 bonus, too. He and his wife and two teenage children
live in a house that he figures is worth $500,000, and his
mortgage payments, local real-estate taxes, and other deductions come to $50,700 a year. His investment portfolio of
stocks produced $40,000 in long-term capital gains last year.
How would he make out under the current law versus the
flat tax?

Our hypothetical executive had some gains and some
losses under the change to the flat-tax system. First, he got to
keep that $40,000 of capital gains in its entirety, because it
isn't taxed under the flat tax. But he lost a lot of deductions.
Don't despair for our executive. The rate is what counts for
him. Even with a higher taxable income, his tax bill is slashed

nearly 50 percent under a 17 percent flat tax. The $107,955 he would pay under our current tax code plunges to just $54,162 under the 17 percent tax—and even under the Treasury's 20.8 percent rate, he saves a whopping $41,686—a 39 percent tax cut. You think he likes the flat tax?

EXAMPLE 2

$350,000 Wages (Including Bonus)

Married Taxpayers

Total Income	$ 390,000
Wages	$ 350,000
Capital Gains (Losses)	$ 40,000
Interest & Dividends	$ —
Home Mortgage Interest Paid	$ 15,600
Charitable Contributions	$ 11,700
Other Itemized Deductions	$ 23,400
Number of Children	2

	Tax under current law	A revenue-neutral flat tax at 20.8%	Tax under Armey-Shelby-type 17% flat tax
Net tax liability	$107,955	$66,269	$54,162
Increase or decrease from present law		−$41,686	−$53,793
% increase or decrease from present law		−39%	−50%

But wait a minute. Our executive gets tired of living in the wintry Northeast and decides he's going to move the family to Southern California. He calls up a real-estate agent to talk about selling his suburban mini-mansion and gets the bad news: housing demand is terrible. Ever since the flat tax ended mortgage deductions, it has become horribly difficult to sell a house.

"People used to buy houses because the federal government subsidized the mortgage and real-estate taxes," explains the agent. "Why would anybody want to buy a house when they can rent it cheaper and not have to worry about all the maintenance?"

"Well, I figure the house is worth at least $500,000," says the executive. "What should we ask for it?"

"You'll be lucky to get $375,000," she says, "and you'll have to throw in the Lexus if you want that. Otherwise, don't count on more than $350,000."

Ugh. Our man hadn't counted on taking such a big hit on his house. After all, he planned to use the equity in this house to buy that fancy house in the mountains above the Los Angeles smog. Maybe that flat tax isn't such a good idea.

But then again that house in California might not be as expensive as it once was, either. Maybe he'll have enough for the down payment after all. This is getting confusing.

As you can see, there may be many tradeoffs involved in evaluating the flat tax. It's impossible to know precisely how house prices would be affected by a flat tax that ends the deduction for mortgage interest and real-estate taxes. For example, it may surprise you to learn that less than one fourth of all individual tax returns filed for 1993 showed a deduction for mortgage interest. Thus, the importance of this deduction, which was created to encourage home ownership, may be vastly exaggerated in the public mind. But then again, there are a lot of young people out there diligently saving to buy their first house and they may like the idea of being able eventually to have the government subsidize that house purchase.

THE FLAT TAX: A BIG FAMILY

Let's look at a group that, for the most part, seems to get a big break under the flat tax: families at the upper end of the Middle American salary range. Under the flat-tax proposals being discussed, there are generous exemptions that are designed to protect the poor from paying any income tax. But those exemptions are so generous that they also help even high-income Americans with big families shelter pretty good chunks of money from taxes. Couple that with the lower rates under the flat-tax proposals, and it appears that the flat tax is very good to families.

THE SIXERS TAXES

Here's an example in which we have a family of six. The father earns $200,000 a year; the family lives in a big five-bedroom house worth $400,000 and pays mortgage interest of $14,350. Rearing four children has been expensive, so there hasn't been a lot of money to invest. As a result, the family receives only about $5,000 in interest and dividend income each year.

EXAMPLE 3

$200,000 HOMEOWNER

Married Taxpayers

Total Income	$	205,000
Wages	$	200,000
Capital Gains (Losses)	$	–
Interest & Dividends	$	5,000
Home Mortgage Interest Paid	$	14,350
Charitable Contributions	$	4,100
Other Itemized Deductions	$	18,450
Number of Children		4

	Tax under current law	A revenue-neutral flat tax at 20.8%	Tax under Armey-Shelby-type 17% flat tax
Net tax liability	$41,655	$32,989	$26,962
Increase or decrease from present law		−$8,666	−$14,693
% increase or decrease from present law		−21%	−35%

THE RENTERS' TAXES

But what happens to a similar family of six, with the same income from salaries and investments and the same contributions, that rents a nice house in the suburbs instead of owning it?

So big families with good incomes do well under the flat tax, although renters do better than homeowners because they don't lose the mortgage-interest or property-tax deductions. That suggests that the mortgage deduction under the current tax system is indeed a powerful incentive to own a home.

EXAMPLE 4

$200,000 RENTERS

Married Taxpayers

Total income	$ 205,000
Wages	$ 200,000
Capital Gains (Losses)	$ –
Interest & Dividends	$ 5,000
Home Mortgage Interest Paid	$ –
Charitable Contributions	$ 4,100
Other Itemized Deductions	$ 14,350
Number of Children	4

	Tax under current law	A revenue-neutral flat tax at 20.8%	Tax under Armey-Shelby-type 17% flat tax
Net tax liability	$48,297	$32,989	$26,962
Increase or decrease from present law		−$15,308	−$21,335
% increase or decrease from present law		−32%	−44%

THE DINKYS

Now let's switch gears and examine the impact of a flat tax on some other high-income people. We'll start with what has come to be known as Dinkys, or DINKs ("double incomes, no kids"). Let's give our married couple some high-paying jobs: she earns $110,000 as an accountant, he earns $90,000 as a public-relations executive. They own a condominium worth $250,000 and pay mortgage interest of $18,000 annually. Our couple enjoy the good life, eating out often and taking great vacations, but they've also been careful about investing. Last year they were paid $8,000 in interest and dividends and realized $15,000 more in capital gains from the sale of a hot stock they had owned for a few years. Charitable contributions aren't part of their lifestyle.

EXAMPLE 5

The Dinkys

Married Taxpayers

Total Income	$ 223,000
Wages	$ 200,000
Capital Gains (Losses)	$ 15,000
Interest & Dividends	$ 8,000
Home Mortgage Interest Paid	$ 18,000
Charitable Contributions	$ —
Other Itemized Deductions	$ 13,380
Number of Children	—

	Tax under current law	A revenue-neutral flat tax at 20.8%	Tax under Armey-Shelby-type 17% flat tax
Net tax liability	$52,274	$37,149	$30,362
Increase or decrease from present law		−$15,126	−$21,912
% increase or decrease from present law		−29%	−42%

Well, the Dinkys certainly make out well under a flat tax, saving nearly $22,000 in tax payments under the 17 percent flat tax. Unless, of course, the value of that condo comes tumbling down with the elimination of the mortgage interest deduction.

SINGLE SANDRA

Meet another well-paid taxpayer, Single Sandra. Sandra works at an advertising agency where she's a top account executive pulling down $180,000. No kids, no commitments. She rents a luxury apartment, travels extensively, and spends lavishly. Her parents left her $75,000 that she has invested for the long run in stocks; she gets only $2,000 in dividends, but is counting on that stock portfolio to grow at a 10 percent annual rate to finance an early retirement. How does she fare under the flat tax?

EXAMPLE 6

SINGLE SANDRA

Single Taxpayers

Total Income	$ 182,000
Wages	$ 180,000
Capital Gains (Losses)	$ —
Interest & Dividends	$ 2,000
Home Mortgage Interest Paid	$ —
Charitable Contributions	$ 3,640
Other Itemized Deductions	$ 16,380
Number of Children	—

	Tax under current law	A revenue-neutral flat tax at 20.8%	Tax under Armey-Shelby-type 17% flat tax
Net tax liability	$47,634	$35,214	$28,781
Increase or decrease from present law		−$12,420	−$18,853
% increase or decrease from present law		−26%	−40%

THE FERRY FAMILY

The last in our high-income taxpayers is a charming couple, Harry and Mary Ferry. Harry, age seventy-one, retired five years ago after a successful career as a sales rep. Mary never worked, spending all her time rearing their two children, who have long since moved away, with careers and lives of their own. The Ferrys own their house—a four-bedroom suburban home on a nice lot—outright. Harry's pension pays $70,000 a year, and they have $35,000 in annual income from a bond

EXAMPLE 7

THE FERRYS

Married Taxpayers

Total Income	$ 105,000
Wages/Pensions	$ 70,000
Capital Gains (Losses)	$ –
Interest & Dividends	$ 35,000
Home Mortgage Interest Paid	$ –
Charitable Contributions	$ 3,500
Other Itemized Deductions	$ 9,450
Number of Children	–

	Tax under current law	A revenue-neutral flat tax at 20.8%	Tax under Armey-Shelby-type 17% flat tax
Net tax liability	$19,133	$10,109	$8,262
Increase or decrease from present law		−$9,024	−$10,871
% increase or decrease from present law		−47%	−57%

portfolio. Church and other charitable contributions total $3,500 annually.

The Ferry family comes out way ahead under a flat tax. After all, they didn't have any mortgage interest deduction to lose so the switch to a flat tax was mostly gravy for them. Only one little glitch might worry the Ferrys. If, as flat-taxers argue, interest rates fall sharply, the Ferrys may find over time that their bond portfolio is giving them less interest income than it did before. But that shouldn't be too big a worry. The interest income won't fall far enough to wipe out that $10,871 extra they get to keep under the 17 percent flat tax.

Well, there you have it for the upper crust: a 17 percent flat tax would save these taxpayers large amounts of money. The loss of the mortgage-interest deduction would hurt, sure. But it wouldn't hurt *that* much. These folks only need to worry about what happens when they sell that house. Maybe, as the flat-taxers argue, everything will be just fine and lower interest rates will offset the loss of the mortgage-interest deduction, allowing homeowners to retain most of their equity in those houses. But that is a big question mark.

THE FLAT TAX AND MIDDLE AMERICA: THE GREAT UNKNOWN

Now we come to the battlefield where the fight for the flat tax will be won or lost. These are the people who ultimately will decide whether we want or don't want a flat tax, or even a major overhaul of our tax system. Needless to say, there are a lot of different kinds of people inhabiting this category: Midwestern farmers, young Wall Street executives, retirees, big families, and single wage earners. Some will own houses while others rent. Some will make a lucrative hobby of investing and others will spend every penny they earn on vacations, clothes, and restaurant meals. In short, it is very difficult to characterize how a flat tax will affect this broad swath of our population. Every situation will be different. We're giving you several different examples of the impact of a flat tax to demonstrate how complex such a change would be.

EXAMPLE 8

The Foursome Family

Married Taxpayers

Total Income	$ 75,000
Wages	$ 70,500
Capital Gains (Losses)	$ 1,500
Interest & Dividends	$ 3,000
Home Mortgage Interest Paid	$ 6,000
Charitable Contributions	$ 1,500
Other Itemized Deductions	$ 6,000
Number of Children	2

	Tax under current law	A revenue-neutral flat tax at 20.8%	Tax under Armey-Shelby-type 17% flat tax
Net tax liability	$9,151	$8,133	$6,647
Increase or decrease from present law		−$1,018	−$2,504
% increase or decrease from present law		−11%	−27%

A FAMILY OF FOUR

Consider a married couple with two dependent children and a total income of $75,000, consisting of $70,500 in salary, $1,500 in long-term capital gains, and $3,000 in dividends and interest. They have itemized deductions totaling $13,500. See Example 8.

The Foursomes do okay under a 17 percent plan, gaining about $2,500 in tax savings. But note that the savings is slashed to just $1,000 at the Treasury's flat-tax rate of 20.8 percent. The benefits of a flat tax are starting to fade.

THE REAL MIDDLE OF MIDDLE AMERICA

Now let's bring those earnings down to the level of Average America, ranging from $45,000 to $60,000. First, we'll compare a $60,000-a-year family of six that owns a home to a similar family that rents.

The Homeowners, you will see in Example 9, have reason to be very pleased. They came out way ahead even with the loss of the mortgage-interest deduction. See Example 10 for the same scenario for the Renters.

EXAMPLE 9

The Homeowners

Married Taxpayers

Total Income	$ 60,000
Wages	$ 58,200
Capital Gains (Losses)	$ 600
Interest & Dividends	$ 1,200
Home Mortgage Interest Paid	$ 4,200
Charitable Contributions	$ 1,200
Other Itemized Deductions	$ 4,200
Number of Children	4

	Tax under current law	A revenue-neutral flat tax at 20.8%	Tax under Armey-Shelby-type 17% flat tax
Net tax liability	$5,265	$3,494	$2,856
Increase or decrease from present law		−$1,771	−$2,409
% increase or decrease from present law		−34%	−46%

The Renters

There's an even bigger win for the Renters: a total reduction in their tax bill of 50 percent, a savings of more than $2,800. Example 10, combined with the Homeowners' above, shows us that at the average middle-class income level of $60,000, the mortgage-interest deduction is small enough that the pride of ownership, as opposed to renting, can inspire many people to buy a house, with or without the mortgage-interest deduction.

EXAMPLE 10

The Renters

Married Taxpayers

Total Income	$ 60,000
Wages	$ 58,200
Capital Gains (Losses)	$ 600
Interest & Dividends	$ 1,200
Home Mortgage Interest Paid	$ –
Charitable Contributions	$ 1,200
Other Itemized Deductions	$ 4,200
Number of Children	4

	Tax under current law	A revenue-neutral flat tax at 20.8%	Tax under Armey-Shelby-type 17% flat tax
Net tax liability	$5,700	$3,494	$2,856
Increase or decrease from present law		−$2,206	−$2,844
% increase or decrease from present law		−39%	−50%

The Middle-Class Dinkys

But let's look at another American family that isn't exactly rare: the middle-class Dinkys. We'll assume that unlike the well-off Dinkys we met earlier, these two are working at secure jobs—they are both schoolteachers—that don't pay particularly well. They have just bought a new house and have some hefty mortgage payments. But remember that this example could just as easily be an older couple whose kids are grown and who have moved to Florida. The point is, there are lots of people out there who might fit this example.

EXAMPLE 11

$60,000 No Kids

Married Taxpayers

Total Income	$ 60,000
Wages	$ 60,000
Capital Gains (Losses)	$ –
Interest & Dividends	$ –
Home Mortgage Interest Paid	$ 8,400
Charitable Contributions	$ 1,200
Other Itemized Deductions	$ 4,200
Number of Children	–

	Tax under current law	A revenue-neutral flat tax at 20.8%	Tax under Armey-Shelby-type 17% flat tax
Net tax liability	$6,295	$8,029	$6,562
Increase or decrease from present law		+$1,734	+$267
% increase or decrease from present law		+28%	+4%

Ouch! The flat tax just cost the Dinkys $267 more than they would pay under the current tax system. And what if Congress decides that the 17 percent rate just isn't high enough to fund government and decides to go with the Treasury's 20.8 percent rate? Bam! Now the Dinkys are scrambling to dig up $1,734 more to meet the tax levy under the flat-tax system. That wasn't pleasant. If you are trying to sell the Armey-Shelby flat tax, you might not knock on this family's door. They probably won't be too enthusiastic.

THE $45,000 FAMILY OF FOUR

Here we have an older factory worker with a wife and two kids. They've put together a modest investment program, but his salary is what keeps this family afloat.

EXAMPLE 12

FACTORY WORKER FAMILY

Married Taxpayers

Total Income	$ 46,436
Wages	$ 45,000
Capital Gains (Losses)	$ 479
Interest & Dividends	$ 957
Home Mortgage Interest Paid	$ 3,351
Charitable Contributions	$ 957
Other Itemized Deductions	$ 3,351
Number of Children	2

	Tax under current law	A revenue-neutral flat tax at 20.8%	Tax under Armey-Shelby-type 17% flat tax
Net tax liability	$4,286	$2,720	$2,312
Increase or decrease from present law		−$1,567	−$1,975
% increase or decrease from present law		−37%	−46%

This is more like it. Now the flat tax is back in favor since it grants some substantial tax savings for this family. The rate under the current tax code is just 15 percent, but taxable income is much larger.

The $45,000 Single

We're back to our Single Sandra, but now she earns $45,000 instead of the $182,000 income we gave her earlier. Let's compare her situation to the Factory family.

EXAMPLE 13

$45,000 No Complications

Single Taxpayers

Total Income	$	45,000
Wages	$	45,000
Capital Gains (Losses)	$	–
Interest & Dividends	$	–
Home Mortgage Interest Paid	$	–
Charitable Contributions	$	–
Other Itemized Deductions	$	–
Number of Children		–

	Tax under current law	A revenue-neutral flat tax at 20.8%	Tax under Armey-Shelby-type 17% flat tax
Net tax liability	$7,646	$7,134	$5,831
Increase or decrease from present law		–$512	–$1,815
% increase or decrease from present law		–7%	–24%

Sandra doesn't fare as well under the 17 percent flat tax as the Factory family, but she's still considerably better off with more than $1,800 in additional spending money left after taxes. Once again, though, if the Treasury rate of 20.8 percent is adopted instead of 17 percent, Sandra's tax benefits shrink considerably to just over $500.

What, then, are we to make of a flat-tax plan for Middle America? On balance, based on the Deloitte calculations, most of our hypothetical taxpayers are better off under a flat-tax plan. But the margin of gains narrows considerably from those enjoyed by their wealthier neighbors. And some people come off worse. The mortgage-interest deduction clearly benefits wealthier taxpayers more than it does the middle class, but even at the higher ends of the middle-class income range, it is valuable. And that raises an interesting question. If politicians decide that the home mortgage interest deduction really is sacred and decide to preserve it, they presumably will have to make up the lost tax revenue by raising rates some. Clearly, there are cases where the modest tax benefits of a flat tax at 17 percent or 20.8 percent would become modest liabilities at 22 percent or 25 percent. Since we can virtually guarantee you that Congress will keep fiddling with the tax code even after a flat-tax plan is adopted, that's something to think about.

LOW-INCOME AMERICA

Nobody wants to hurt low-income Americans. Both the current tax law and the flat-tax proposals that are being floated try to protect low-income citizens from the burden of income taxes. But as we've seen, the flat-tax system provides much more generous protection for lower incomes. So it might seem at first glance as though the flat tax should be welcome news for many low-income taxpayers.

But wait! We haven't yet dealt with the earned-income tax credit. This is a feature in the current tax law designed to help low-income workers that the flat-tax plan doesn't have. And it can make a big difference to some low-income wage earners. The credit, created in 1975, was designed to help the working poor by either reducing the amount of taxes owed or, more importantly, giving workers who don't owe any tax a cash payment. To get the credit, though, you must file a tax return, even if you don't owe a penny or even if you didn't earn enough money to file a return.

Proponents say the credit is a critically important anti-poverty program. Critics call it a farce, arguing that it is far too vulnerable to fraud.

Consider a single mother with two kids and an income of $10,000. Suppose the worker had only $9,500 in wages, $100 in long-term capital gains, and $400 in interest and dividends. Under current law, thanks to the earned-income tax credit, the worker would *receive* $2,481 from Uncle Sam. Under the flat tax, assuming that the earned-income tax credit is eliminated, the worker wouldn't get that fat check. So don't count on her to campaign for an Armey-Shelby-type flat tax.

Giving Treasury a Say

So now you think we're all through with demonstrating how a flat-tax plan would affect you and your friends?

Wrong!

To demonstrate yet again how complex all this stuff can be—and, not coincidentally, to keep the Treasury Department from hounding us—we're going to give you a summary of why Treasury officials are adamant in predicting that a flat-tax plan at 20.8 percent (Treasury's estimate of the rate necessary to be revenue neutral) is going to result in *rising* income taxes for most of Middle America.

The Treasury analysis provides detailed examples of the impact of a 20.8 percent flat tax on six "typical families." The important thing about the Treasury analysis, though, is that it makes some assumptions of its own about how businesses would pass along their higher tax burdens to the rest of us. While some economists agree with the Treasury's methods, others are dubious.

At the same time, the Treasury questions assumptions made by the flat-tax proponents that interest rates will fall significantly and that economic activity will surge as a result of a flat tax. As you will see in the essay by Deputy Treasury Secretary Lawrence Summers in chapter 9, the Treasury is dubious about nearly all the supposed benefits of the flat tax.

Just remember: nobody knows for sure.

Here are the Treasury's examples:

❑ The total tax burden for a single worker earning $8,840 a year would drop by $152 because the proposal provides higher standard deductions than current law.

❑ The total tax burden for a married couple earning $17,680 with two children would rise by $2,442, "primarily because the proposal would repeal the earned-income tax credit."

❑ The total tax burden on a married couple with $50,000 of wages, two children, and employer-provided health insurance would rise by $1,604. That's because "the taxation of employer-provided health insurance and the employer's contributions to FICA at the business level would more than offset lower taxes on money wages," Treasury says. "Employees would bear the burden in the form of either lower wages, reduced health-insurance benefits, or substitution of taxable wages for formerly tax-exempt health benefits."

❑ The total tax burden for a two-earner married couple with two children, $100,000 of total wages ($50,000 per wage earner), employer-provided health insurance, and $4,000 of investment income would increase by $2,683. That's primarily because of "the effects of taxes on the employer's contributions to FICA and health insurance."

❑ The total tax burden for families with two children and with an income of $212,100 (including investment income) would drop under a flat tax because the tax plan "would exempt investment income of individuals from tax and flatten the rate structure. The total tax burden for a two-earner married couple with each spouse earning $100,000 and a total of $12,100 of investment income would decrease $3,469, even after taking into account the proposal's tax on the employers' contributions to health insurance and FICA. A one-earner couple with the same total income, but a larger share of investment income ($159,100 in wages and $53,000 of investment income) would have a tax reduction of $10,943 for the same reasons."

Naturally, House Majority Leader Armey takes strong exception to the Treasury's calculations. In January 1996, Armey said there is a good word to describe the Treasury's latest analysis of his flat-tax proposal: "fiction." He also said the Treasury's assumptions are based on "assumptions that are false, misleading or at odds with the empirical research of the nation's leading public finance economists."

Armey points out that his plan calls for a 20 percent rate

for the first two years, only slightly below the Treasury's estimated revenue-neutral rate, and that spending cuts could make up the $40 billion difference. The House majority leader also says the Treasury ignores any changes in compliance costs and compliance rates that would come from a flat tax. And he contends that the Treasury analysis "greatly overstates" the amount that employers contribute to the typical health-care plan.

So Armey strongly disputes Treasury's contention that his plan would impose higher taxes on middle-income families. For example, he says his plan would result in a *reduction* of $1,376 in the total tax burden for a typical family of four earning $50,000 a year. After five years, the benefits of the Armey-Shelby flat-tax plan "are even more pronounced," Armey says.

Asked for comment about Armey's countercharges, Treasury officials hold their ground. They say their numbers are the right ones, that Armey is all wet, and that the middle class will be big losers under a flat-tax regime.

Still think this flat-tax idea is simple?

Chapter Five

BUSINESS AND THE FLAT TAX

So far we've seen how a flat tax might create big changes for all sorts of people, both in their tax bills and in other aspects of their lives. Even bigger changes would be in store for American businesses, both large and small, if a flat-tax system is approved. One of the biggest changes would be that the corner grocer and your own dentist, both of whom enjoy their own tax status as small businessmen or professional corporations, would be placed in the same category as IBM and General Electric.

Under the Hall-Rabushka plan, businesses would fill out a ten-line tax return that could be filed on a postcard. That same form would apply to IBM, Microsoft, and Mobil as well as to your corner grocery store or your family physician. Even if you just rent out a room to someone, you would have to fill out the form. So would anyone who is self-employed.

But as with the personal income tax, the simplicity of the business tax stops right after the postcard return. Armies of tax consultants and advisers already are trying to figure out the impact of a switch to any of the different flat-tax plans: what types of businesses would benefit, what types would disappear, how businesses might adapt, how business-financing techniques would be affected, and what transition rules might be needed to soften the impact. This subject really gets us into deep water. Glance through just a few of the thick studies that already have been published, and it quickly becomes obvious that nobody knows what the real impact will be.

Whatever the outcome, many Americans may be surprised to learn how little corporations now pay as a percentage of the nation's total tax collections in recent decades. Ask a few friends what percentage they think comes from corporations. If they are like our friends, most will probably say somewhere between 50 percent and 75 percent. Wrong! In 1994 business income taxes contributed just 11.9 percent of total federal tax revenue. That is only about half the level of about three decades ago.

Here is a look at how the flat-tax system outlined by Hall and Rabushka would work, along with a summary of the major pluses and minuses that tax analysts see. This chapter will also summarize a few reports that have tried to peer into the future and gauge the impact of a flat tax on American business.

HOW A FLAT TAX ON BUSINESS WOULD WORK

The first line of the Hall-Rabushka business income-tax form would show your business's revenues. This would include what your business received from selling or exchanging its products or services produced in the United States or passing through U.S. borders. It would also include money the business received from selling plants, equipment, and land.

What about U.S. businesses that operate all around the globe? Under the Hall-Rabushka plan, the tax would apply only to the U.S. revenues of a business, whether that business is owned by Americans, foreigners, or some combination.

Then you move to line 2, where you get to subtract "allowable costs." These include what you actually paid in goods, services, and materials to make whatever it is your business produces. Allocable costs include wages, salaries, and contributions to pension plans for workers. (But any fringe benefits, such as health-insurance coverage, that your business gave to your workers would not be deductible.) In addition, you would be allowed to subtract all your purchases of equipment, buildings, and "capital equipment" in the United States. That's right—100 percent of what you paid could be deducted in the first year, rather than spreading the cost over future years. Tax geeks refer to this as "expensing." In other words, forget about all those complex depreciation rules and schedules. However—and this is a very big however—you would no longer be allowed to deduct interest payments.

Add up all your costs and put them on line 3. Then subtract all those costs from your revenues, and you are left with your taxable income on line 4. Multiply by 19 percent, and that's your tax, which goes on line 5. Simple as that.

This is not, as Messrs. Hall and Rabushka are quick to point out, a tax on profits. Many businesses with huge profits might owe little or no tax under this system if they are making massive investments in new equipment and buildings. Those massive investments might even give them "negative taxable income." The Hall-Rabushka plan would allow businesses to carry over such amounts into future years, reducing what a business would owe in those years. There wouldn't be any limit to how many years a business could carry forward these amounts, and any such balances would earn interest.

But if revenue from abroad isn't part of this system, wouldn't this encourage American businesses and workers to move abroad? Absolutely not, Messrs. Hall and Rabushka reply, because a 19 percent flat-tax rate would be a powerful incentive for businesses to move here. It would make the vast American market far more attractive, not less attractive.

Advocates say the system's simplicity would greatly benefit business and workers. It would simplify recordkeeping and would cut down on the number of costly disputes between the Internal Revenue Service and corporate tax managers. Moreover, the system clearly rewards businesses that are investing in the future by purchasing new equipment and expanding their plants. And the flat 19 percent rate itself that Messrs. Hall and Rabushka advocate would also be highly appealing.

Flat-tax enthusiasts say this system could be a business lifesaver. They see it as a long-overdue housecleaning, a cleansing of a Byzantine system that even top corporate executives can't understand or analyze. They view the flat tax as a way to reduce or even eliminate the vast numbers of expensive tax lawyers, accountants, and other advisers companies now need to consult before making any important business decisions. Some view a flat tax as a way to boost the overall economy, encourage entrepreneurship, promote savings, and improve the nation's standard of living, enhancing America's stature in the world economy.

In short, flat-tax enthusiasts make it sound as though everybody wins. But many successful business leaders can't help wondering about the question we have raised so frequently in theses pages: What if the flat-taxers are wrong?

THE CRITICS SHOOT BACK

Some government officials fear a flat tax might put many businesses out of business in a hurry, or at least make them much less competitive, and torpedo America's economic future. Listen, for example, to Deputy Treasury Secretary Lawrence H. Summers. In a speech at a Brookings Institution tax conference in 1996, he said the flat tax "could very likely be very burdensome" for many businesses. "I am told that there are many corporate treasurers who have not been pleased when they have filled out the postcard that their companies would need to send to the IRS under a flat tax." (See chapter 9 for a condensed version of his remarks.)

For example, businesses that depend heavily on borrowed money would no longer be able to deduct those interest payments. As Summers pointed out, a tax system that doesn't allow interest to be deducted could mean the difference between prosperity and disaster for the corner grocery store that finances its inventory with bank loans, or for a heavily mortgaged wholesale concern operating on a very thin margin.

Home builders wonder if elimination of the mortgage-interest deduction would ruin them and other related industries. Is it really fair, they ask, to change such basic rules that Americans have relied on for generations and reasonably expected to remain in place in future generations? They also wonder whether it is fair to eliminate deductions for fringe benefits, such as health insurance, and whether this might lead to more Americans being uninsured.

Then there is the delicate problem of what, if anything, to do about businesses that have amassed huge amounts of deductions, credits, and other items over the years under existing law that haven't yet been used. Would they suddenly lose all that? Or would Washington feel obliged to agree to develop transition-relief rules that would be phased gradually over time? Many tax experts agree that it would be politically impossible simply to dump the old system and impose a new system without any transition rules. Several flat-tax advocates also endorse the idea of transition rules to ease the pain. But, naturally, any such relief would result in less revenue, requiring a higher tax rate in order for the plan to be revenue-neutral.

Figuring out how to write transition rules could well be the undoing of the movement to tear up the current system and replace it with something completely new. In theory, transition rules may seem relatively easy to write. But in practice, they can be remarkably difficult and extremely controversial. "When I think about issues relating to the transition to a flat tax," said Deputy Treasury Secretary Summers, "I am reminded of Chairman Mao's assertion that the Cultural Revolution was just a transition problem."

Summers and others have zeroed in on the problem facing many companies that have unused depreciation deductions for past investments.

"What is to be done that is both simple and fair with the $3 trillion in depreciation deductions that lie ahead for past investments in physical capital?" Summers asked. "If these are simply wiped away, the playing field will be completely unfair for those who make (an) investment tomorrow to compete with those who invested yesterday. If some scheme is found for permitting these deductions, extremely complex rules would be necessary whenever assets are transferred. And, in any event, the low rates promised by flat-tax advocates would start to rise."

Naturally, even the simple flat-tax system would not eliminate all thorny questions. Treasury officials are quick to point out that a flat-tax system would not simplify the sticky question of how to differentiate between an "independent contractor" and an employee, a question that long has plagued many small businesses. There would still be many questions about taxpayers who own cars and how to distinguish between personal and business use of those cars. There would still be questions about the rules on deducting an office at home.

Treasury officials are deeply concerned by proposals that would exempt income from foreign operations of U.S. companies. For example, they worry that such a plan would not prevent companies from juggling their books and transferring profits to companies they own in tax-free or low-tax nations.

Banks, insurance companies, and other financial institutions pose especially tricky problems. The Hall-Rabushka book offers a solution, but critics say this is one of the murkiest areas in the corporate-tax world.

Possible Winners and Losers

As we have explained in previous chapters, it is impossible to know for sure exactly who would come out on top and who would be flattened if Washington approved a major new tax law to replace the existing system. Businesses and individuals can be highly creative and flexible. They can adapt to new situations and take advantage of new opportunities. Furthermore, some of the most widely feared effects that critics envision may be short-lived; it is important to consider the possibility of short-term pain leading to longer-term gain.

One goal of a consumption tax—discouraging spending and promoting savings—raises an obvious concern for many businesses that sell consumer goods or help finance the purchase of those goods. Among these would be retailers, consumer-credit companies, makers of consumer goods, and other providers of consumer goods and services, according to a Deloitte & Touche publication. But if the flat tax leads to lower interest rates and stronger economic growth, as flat-taxers confidently predict, then these industries may have little or nothing to fear.

Other big borrowers would feel the impact of elimination of the interest deduction. But it is very difficult to generalize, even among industries, because companies can differ so widely in their financial structure and in many other aspects. Still, it does seem fair to conclude that the world of corporate finance would change radically. A flat tax would make it much more expensive for companies to raise money in the bond markets or by borrowing money from other sources. Thus we might expect to see a shift toward new stock issues coming to market to finance business even as the issuance of corporate bonds declined.

Even as the flat-tax proposals are being debated, corporate-tax wizards are hard at work figuring out how they might get around them. Several tax lawyers have warned us that the flat tax would greatly increase the incentive to convert regular income into capital gains, and that there are many clever ways in which this could be done. Naturally, the Treasury could write anti-abuse rules to combat any such efforts, but anti-abuse rules typically are not simple. That is why some people quip that if anyone tries to put all the necessary rules and instructions on a postcard, you would need an electron microscope to read them.

Chapter Six

THE TAX
INFRASTRUCTURE

The scrapping of our current tax system and the adoption of a flat tax plainly would have a huge impact on American society. While many people have enthusiastically applauded the simplicity of proposals by Steve Forbes, Representative Armey, and Senator Shelby, those plans clearly would cause big trouble for many individuals and organizations. Chief among these would be the legions of highly trained tax lawyers, accountants, and other advisers who serve both ordinary taxpayers as well as businesses. For tax specialists, complexity typically is beautiful. A simpler tax code could also spell trouble for many employees of the Internal Revenue Service. If we move to a much simpler system, would we really need more than 114,000 IRS workers? It is also fair to assume that tax-preparation services such as H&R Block would be forced to radically alter the nature of their business or face extinction. The immense tax-exempt bond business probably would undergo wrenching changes. And, of course, the housing industry, from real-estate agents to carpenters, would confront at best an uncertain future. Finally, many charities and cultural institutions might find their flow of funds sharply curtailed under a tax law that makes each dollar given to charity much more expensive for the wealthy to give than it is now.

Nobody knows exactly what the ultimate outcome of such a massive shift would be for these people and organizations. But because the current tax code has been at least partly responsible for creating the jobs these people hold and for encouraging the goals to which the organizations devote themselves, it's worth thinking about some "what ifs?"

WILL A FLAT TAX SILENCE GLYNN?

Glynn Mapes is a colleague of ours at *The Wall Street Journal* and he's terrified by the thought of a flat tax. Glynn, you see, is a fine amateur singer and a member of the highly regarded Collegiate Chorale in New York City. He's convinced that a flat tax that ends the deduction for charitable giving—and eliminates estate taxes—would mean the end of the Collegiate Chorale, which depends on such giving for a significant portion of its annual budget. Glynn isn't alone. All across the country, charitable organizations, ranging from the multifaceted United Way to local soup kitchens that feed the homeless, are worrying about any proposal that might make their already difficult job of raising funds more difficult.

To see if Glynn's concern is justified, let's walk through some of the economics of charity. Under our current law, you are allowed to deduct gifts to all qualified groups, although the amount of the deduction you may take is phased out gradually once your income rises above certain levels. In essence, the income-tax rules of today effectively cut the net cost, or the true price, of a gift. Or, to put it another way, the current tax code provides a significant incentive for many people to donate.

So what would happen if that law suddenly changed? As we saw in the previous chapter "Who Wins? Who Loses?", most wealthy people would get huge reductions in their tax bills under the flat-tax proposals being bandied about. Thus, they might be more able and willing to make gifts to charity. In that case, no problem. Glynn gets to keep singing.

But maybe the loss of the charitable-gift deduction will make some donors think twice about giving, or at least about making smaller gifts. Instead of a big donor dashing off a check for $100,000, that donor might only give $50,000. Or nothing at all. If enough people think like that, something would have to give, and it may be that the Collegiate Chorale or the local soup kitchen folds.

Which scenario would it be? Some experts who have studied this issue say it is very tough to generalize because there are so many different types of nonprofit organizations. Also, reactions are likely to differ depending on income levels. It's worth remembering that about 70 percent of all returns take the standard deduction; thus, those taxpayers can't deduct their gifts at all under current law. Besides, many people say their gift-giving doesn't depend on getting a tax deduction. Elimination of the deduction "would not affect my charitable giving one iota," says David A. Lifson, a New York City certified public accountant and a partner in the firm of Hays & Co. But what about very wealthy philanthropists? Those in the top brackets might well think twice about making certain gifts. So even though taxes clearly are not the only consideration in giving, studies have shown that tax considerations can and do affect *how much* some people give.

Some groups, though, would be much less affected than others. Take churches, for example. The impact of a flat tax might be milder on churches than on other nonprofit organizations. This point is borne out by a recent study by Charles T. Clotfelter and Richard L. Schmalbeck of Duke University. (Clotfelter is a professor of public policy studies and economics, while Schmalbeck is a law professor.) In a paper they presented at a Brookings Institution conference in Washington, they pointed out that most people do not itemize their deductions. They also pointed out that because lower-bracket taxpayers tend to favor religious groups in making donations, it follows that elimination of the deduction "would likely cause only modest erosion of contributed support to religious organizations." But they warned: "Much greater damage may be done to organizations that have traditionally been favored by higher-bracket taxpayers who have benefited from the existing tax incentives." Similarly, groups that depend heavily on corporate donations could feel an instant pinch if those companies could no longer deduct such gifts.

The two professors concluded that at least some of the tax-overhaul proposals, if enacted, "are likely to have significant and adverse effects on nonprofit organizations."

There's another issue worth considering here, though, that goes beyond the economic impact of eliminating the deduction for charitable contributions and it is a question of philosophy. Should the government, through the tax code, encourage its citizens to give a portion of their wealth to charity? Many people and members of Congress answer this question loudly and unequivocally: Yes!

But nonprofit groups' fears may be wildly exaggerated. Some flat-tax advocates argue that any impact would be short-lived and relatively mild, and that over time, deserving activities would not disappear under a flat tax. They say that large amounts of charitable contributions currently are made by people who take the standard deduction on their income tax returns and thus do not benefit from making a charitable contribution. And looking back at the decade of the 1980s they contend that individual giving grew strongly even though marginal income tax rates fell sharply.

If they're right about public behavior, Glynn can keep singing.

Houses, Mortgages, and Taxes

Flat-taxers as home wreckers? Many people in the real-estate industry would certainly have us think so. They spent huge amounts of money on advertisements and leaflets in the 1996 presidential primaries trying to convince homeowners that a flat tax with no provision for mortgage interest or real-estate tax deductions would drive down home prices. Not stated, but clearly implied: it would also dry up their own incomes and jobs.

When real-estate agents and mortgage bankers argue to homeowners that the mortgage-interest deduction should be preserved, they are preaching to the choir. For people fortunate enough to own a home and earn enough money to itemize deductions, the home mortgage interest deduction is an extraordinarily important way to shelter income from taxes. Perhaps more important to many homeowners, however, is the value of their houses. After all, for many homeowners a house is their single largest asset. Anything that threatens the value of that house is a major threat to their financial well-being.

"Houses remain the single most important store of wealth

for much of the population," says Alan Greenspan, chairman of the Federal Reserve Board. Consumers view their home equity "as a cushion against possible hard times." Moreover, many people tap into their home equity for such purposes as home improvements, auto purchases, college tuition, and consolidation of debts. "Home equity lines of credit, rare just ten years ago, are now held by roughly five million homeowners," Greenspan said in a speech in February of 1996.

In reply, flat-tax advocates argue that fears of a real-estate depression are vastly overblown. First, they predict that the Armey-Shelby plan or other similar proposals would help drive down interest rates quickly. Thus, homeowners could refinance their existing houses, and new homeowners could take out mortgages at low rates. While home prices might initially slump somewhat, they wouldn't change much over the long term. The cost of owning a home wouldn't change significantly, real-estate agents could still collect their commissions on sales and homebuilders would continue to erect more houses.

Flat-taxers also point out that even under today's law, many homeowners don't deduct mortgage interest. Most Americans take the standard deduction. IRS statistics show that home mortgage interest was deducted on only 27.2 million individual returns in the 1993 tax year. That was only 24 percent of all individual income-tax returns filled for that year.

Some flat-taxers even take issue with the notion that home values would plunge if the mortgage-interest deduction disappears. Heritage Foundation economists William Beach and Daniel Mitchell contend that the flat tax would actually *increase* home values "by at least 7 percent." They argue that the flat tax would accelerate economic growth significantly, thus causing incomes and consequently home values to increase.

But many real-estate industry executives clearly aren't buying that argument. Neither did three analysts who recently wrote a detailed paper on this subject for the Brookings conference in February 1996. They concluded that elimination of the deduction "generally will cause a significant price decline, especially in areas with high property taxes and high house prices." The three authors are Richard K. Green of the School of Business at the University of Wisconsin-Madison, Patric H. Hendershott of the Max Fisher School of Business at Ohio State University, and Dennis R. Capozza of the School of Business at the University of Michigan.

Other analysts point out that the effect of a flat tax would vary widely. For example, those who take the standard deduction or who own their homes outright would feel little or no immediate pain from the elimination of the mortgage-interest deduction. Only if prices fell and they tried to sell their houses would they be hurt. One former Treasury official we know points out that he doesn't believe he would be affected at all, even if home prices slumped, because he owns his home outright and has no plan to sell. But the story could be very different for someone who buys a home right before the mortgage deduction is eliminated and then is forced to sell shortly thereafter for some reason, such as a transfer to a new location. In short, the impact of scrapping the home mortgage-deduction in exchange for a simple tax system might be considerably more varied and more profound than some people appreciate.

Of course, there are proposals among the various flat-tax

schemes out there to retain the mortgage-interest deduction. Clearly these proposals are aimed at keeping a very vocal and powerful minority of the voting public happy. But at what cost? Retaining the mortgage-interest deduction would obviously reduce the government's revenues and would require a higher flat-tax rate if the plan were to be revenue-neutral. And if you retain the mortgage-interest deduction, pressure inevitably would increase to retain other deductions, too. Saying yes to one group makes it very hard to say no to everyone else. This is a key factor to consider in analyzing the long-term future of a tax system that purports to be fairer than the existing one. Caving in to pressure from real-estate interests and homeowners could mark the first step on the road right back to where we are today: a tax code riddled with exceptions and favors for special-interest groups.

MUNICIPAL BONDS AND TAXES

State and local governments have been watching the flat-tax debate with especially keen interest. Under current law, they can raise money to pay for bridges, tunnels, and other projects at highly attractive rates merely by issuing bonds. Those bonds pay interest that is free of all federal income tax. In many places, state law exempts interest income from in-state bonds from all state and local income taxes, too. For example, if you live in New York City and buy bonds issued by New York State or municipalities within the state, you don't owe any federal, state, or local taxes on the interest income. Because of this exemption, state and local governments typically are able to raise money at even lower interest rates than those the U.S. Treasury must pay when it issues bonds. Interest on Treasury bonds, after all, is fully taxable at the federal level.

So it is easy to see why many state and local government leaders are deeply concerned by any proposals to eliminate taxes on investment income. That, in turn, would remove the incentive for investors to load up on tax-exempt bonds. And that could mean sharply higher borrowing costs for municipalities at a time when they fear federal aid cutbacks and sluggish economic growth that could slow the growth of their tax collections.

Then there is the thorny question of what would happen to the more than $1.2 trillion of bonds that have already been issued over the years. Would Washington dare to scrap the current law without providing any transition rules to ease the pain of investors holding those bonds?

Take a deep breath and calm down, flat-taxers reply. Some say fears of a municipal-bond market debacle are nonsense. They predict that a flat-tax plan would mean Treasury bond yields would fall sharply, bringing those yields down to tax-exempt bond levels. Whether they are right, of course, is anyone's guess. As many academic studies have shown, the bond markets are notoriously unpredictable.

Municipal-finance specialists say they will continue to be needed, whether or not there are tax-exempt bonds. Removing the tax exemption won't change state and local government needs for money to build new bridges, roads, schools, and tunnels, to renovate existing infrastructure, or to construct other projects. However, many municipalities might have to pay more to borrow money than they otherwise would.

THE IRS, TAX LAWYERS, AND ACCOUNTANTS

We don't need to tell you that of all the U.S. institutions that pervade our lives today, the IRS is probably the most hated, feared, and intrusive. Only the frightening—and sometimes bumbling—operations of the Central Intelligence Agency create an emotional sensation to rival that of the IRS, and at least the CIA is supposed to be aiming its agents at America's enemies instead of its citizens. Several tax-overhaul plans are designed to shrink the size of the IRS.

While unemployment never has been one of America's social goals, many people probably would be delighted to see a new tax system that flattens both the IRS and the tax-advisory business. But that may be wishful thinking. Even with the simplest tax code, do not expect the IRS to disappear overnight.

It is hard to imagine any society today whose citizens would willingly cough up all their required taxes without any prodding or checking from Big Brother. IRS officials often compare themselves to traffic cops whose presence by the roadside helps deter speeding. Eliminate all traffic cops, they say, and you would surely see a surge in illegal and dangerous speeding by motorists. Even under some of the simplest tax-overhaul plans, there would still be numerous complex questions to resolve and issues that would require government regulations, as well as scrutiny by tax collectors.

Still, do we really need a tax police force with a budget that exceeds $7 billion and which has a workforce of more than 114,000? Wander through the halls of IRS headquarters in Washington, as we frequently have, and you cannot help but wonder about a tax system that produces so many jobs in so many arcane areas. And that is only the tip of the iceberg. The IRS is a sprawling empire with offices all around the country. Our tax laws are so complex that IRS offices in one city often provide advice that directly contradicts advice in another city.

As tax lawyers are fond of pointing out, many tax questions are so complex that there is often no one correct answer.

Enactment of a radical, simple flat tax could be hazardous to the wealth of many tax lawyers, especially those at small firms that cater to individuals. While the number of tax lawyers has fallen in recent years, the population still is very large. The American Bar Association tax section, for example, says it counted 21,696 members as of September 1995. Then there are huge numbers of accountants, enrolled agents, and other tax advisers, ranging from expensive Park Avenue firms to one-person storefront operations. And don't forget all those tax lobbyists.

What might happen to the ranks of these groups if Washington really got serious about overhauling the tax code? That is a subject many lawyers, accountants, and tax lobbyists tell us they are not losing much sleep over these days. Why get excited about something whose chances are remote, at best? They sound far more worried about the chances of a meteor slamming into this planet than about the possibility of Washington approving a simple flat-tax plan that might eliminate the need for their services. Even if Congress did approve a major tax-simplification bill, wouldn't there be constant pressure to tinker with the new system to benefit this big corporation or that big special interest? Just look at what happened in the decade following the historic 1986 tax act: the top tax rate rose sharply over the following decade. So why should anyone think that voters willingly will give up long-cherished deductions in exchange for politicians' promises to reduce rates and keep them low?

Chapter Seven

The Players

Mention the flat tax, and some people think only of Steve Forbes, who spent a fortune promoting the idea as the center-piece of his presidential bid. Several of our friends and colleagues even have asked why we are bothering to write a book about the flat tax. Does this idea really have much support? Won't the issue fade as surely as the New Hampshire snows melt each spring? It is increasingly fashionable to compare the flat-tax movement with the ill-starred health-care overhaul campaign, an idea that initially sounded highly appealing to many people but quickly ran out of supporters as people began zeroing in on complex details.

Maybe so. But keep in mind that there are many other leading political, academic, and journalistic players determined to keep the flat tax and other tax-overhaul ideas at the forefront in coming years. This message comes not only from flat-tax fans but also from the most vocal critics. Granted, it is very tough to find common ground among tax-overhaul advocates. Proposals to replace the current system range enormously, and when you talk with some of the advocates, it is natural to wonder how they could ever agree on anything. But these proponents do share something in common: they are convinced that the current code is a gigantic mess, that it is keeping the nation from expanding as quickly as it should be, and that the tax system needs to be fixed.

So while history might seem to indicate that the most likely outcome of this debate is inaction, history may not be such a reliable guide this time around. For one thing, public dissatisfaction with today's system runs very deep. For another, some of the most important players, such as House Ways and Means Chairman Bill Archer and Senate Finance Chairman Bill Roth, only recently have risen to power and are significantly different from their predecessors.

Here is a brief look at a few of those new leading players and why the tax-overhaul debate may really just be starting.

TEAR UP THE TAX CODE

In the House, leaders of both parties want to overhaul the code. Majority Leader Dick Armey of Texas enthusiastically backs a flat-tax plan and is promoting it extensively. Minority Leader Dick Gephardt of Missouri, who has a plan of his own, is also a strong critic of today's system. Naturally, there is little agreement between these two about what a new tax system should look like. Armey, for example, says the Gephardt plan is "as flat as the Rocky Mountains."

The Ways and Means Committee is holding a long series of public hearings this year on tax reform, and several members, including the chairman, want to eliminate today's system completely. The chairman of that committee is Bill Archer, a Texas Republican.

While far less known than Republican leaders such as House Speaker Newt Gingrich, House Majority Leader Armey, or Senate Majority Leader Bob Dole, Bill Archer is playing an increasingly prominent role—and enjoying it immensely after having been on the losing side of vote after vote for most of his Washington career, when Republicans were in the minority. On the surface, Bill Archer appears to be Mr. Affability. He greets you with a big smile and a warm handshake. He seems relaxed and comfortable with himself. But he can quickly become stern and very tough when he perceives someone as being uncooperative, as he frequently has demonstrated with his stinging questioning of Treasury officials appearing before his committee.

Archer plainly loathes the current tax system and makes no effort to hide his zeal for changing it. (See his essay in chapter 9.) His goal is to rip the system out by the roots so that it can never grow back again in anything like its present form. Forget about minor tinkering. He hasn't yet said precisely what he wants because he says he wants to hear more testimony at hearings he has scheduled this year. But he has said repeatedly that he favors a "broad-based consumption tax," meaning a tax on spending.

Archer stands out in another important way: He says he does his own tax return. That sets him apart from nearly everyone in government. It also may help explain why he feels so strongly about the present system. Whenever you encounter someone who defends the current system, ask them if they do their tax return. Very often, the answer will be: no, of course not. As we have mentioned previously, about half of all individual income-tax returns now are done by paid preparers. Among those who file Form 1040, the percentage rises sharply to more than 60 percent.

For more than two decades, Bill Archer was a voice in the congressional wilderness. But after the Republican victories in 1994, he suddenly found himself catapulted into the chairmanship. One of his aides recalls talking to him the day after Election Day and beginning the conversation: "Congratulations, Mr. Chairman." He says Archer paused, as if somewhat startled by that new title, and then replied slowly: "I like that sound."

Bill Archer sees the next few years as an important window in which to make historic tax-law changes. He typically wins his congressional races with great ease and often hasn't even had an opponent. Bill Archer came to Congress in 1970, winning election to the seat George Bush had occupied before making an unsuccessful bid for the Senate. He joined the Ways and Means Committee in the early 1970s, when it was headed by the late Wilbur Mills, the Democrat whose knowledge of the tax code was legendary.

Some Democrats on the Ways and Means Committee also are in favor of major tax changes. For example, consider Representative Sam Gibbons of Florida, the ranking Democrat on the committee. Gibbons, who briefly headed the committee after Dan Rostenkowski's departure, says he came to the conclusion long ago that the current system "should be replaced." In its place, he favors a value-added tax system that would replace our current personal and corporate income tax system, as well as most of our payroll taxes. He says the current tax system "has become a maze of complexity. It is widely perceived as unfair. It has not kept pace with the economic realities of the modern global marketplace. It creates economic distortions, thus interfering with economic efficiency and growth. It does not reach the huge underground economy. It has become burdensome to many taxpayers, particularly small businesses who must struggle through a pile of federal tax forms every quarter." Gibbons, who often has exchanged strong words with the Republicans running the committee today, has vigorously applauded Chairman Archer for seeking alternatives to the tax system. He plans to retire from Congress when his term expires.

Representative Benjamin L. Cardin, a Democrat from Maryland, also serves on the Ways and Means Committee and also advocates a comprehensive overhaul of the tax system. Last year, he told the committee that the current system has resisted "repeated, strenuous efforts to simplify and reform" it. In short, concern about the tax code clearly is not a Republican issue. It runs across party lines.

Among the most enthusiastic flat-taxers on the Hill is House Majority Leader Armey. Armey, a former economics professor, plans a major offensive in 1996 to publicize his flat-tax plan with Senator Shelby. He easily won reelection in 1994 from his Texas district. Armey's opposite number in the Senate is Bob Dole, a former Finance Committee chairman who is highly knowledgeable about taxes. Senator Dole hasn't endorsed the flat-tax idea, except to say he thinks the system should generally be flatter, although he does share the view that the tax code is badly broken. See his essay in chapter 9.

THE SENATE

In the Senate, Richard Shelby of Alabama has introduced a companion bill to the Armey plan. Senator Sam Nunn of Georgia, a Democrat, and Senator Pete Domenici of New Mexico, a Republican, have joined forces on behalf of a new tax system. As Senator Nunn puts it, our tax system "needs more than a Band-Aid. It needs a transplant." He adds: "If we are serious about our nation's future, we have to scrap the current tax system and put in its place a system that will work for our people and for our country." In short, however vast their differences, many lawmakers from both parties share a common hatred of today's system and sound eager to try something new.

Bill Archer's opposite number in the Senate also has been in Washington for more than two decades but only recently rose to power in the world of taxes. Senator Bill Roth, a Republican from Delaware, took over as Senate Finance chairman after the sudden resignation of Bob Packwood in 1995. Just as Bill Archer differs sharply from his predecessor, so does Bill Roth. Senator Roth long has advocated tax cuts, while Senator Packwood typically sounded skeptical of tax cuts and, instead, placed much greater emphasis on deficit reduction than on tax cuts. Senator Roth's rise to the chairmanship greatly improves the odds for enacting some kind of expanded retirement-savings accounts. This has long been one of his pet projects. Senator Roth, who was born in July 1921, once said he wouldn't run again after he reached age seventy, but he did anyway and won his last campaign by a wide margin. He isn't up for reelection until the year 2000.

With the help of Representative Archer and Senator Dole, Senator Roth helped win an important victory in 1995 that many small-business groups still remember with deep gratitude. The lawmakers helped win approval for legislation that restored partial deductibility of health-insurance premiums paid by more than 3.2 million self-employed workers.

Some of the strongest proponents of the flat-tax concept are outside government. Among these is Jack Kemp, the former Republican congressman who headed a commission that studied the issue and released a report in early 1996. Kemp, a former football star, sees this issue as one of the most important in our economic future. His commission included a wide range of tax specialists, such as former IRS Commissioner Shirley Peterson and Ohio Treasurer Kenneth Blackwell. The Kemp Commission Report is worth reading, even though it doesn't give many specifics about how a new system might work.

Many well-known economists strongly endorse doing away with today's system. One of the strongest flat-tax proponents is Milton Friedman, the Nobel Prize–winning economist and one of the most formidable debating opponents in the nation. Friedman is not only a brilliant and original thinker but also a highly persuasive writer, and he has devoted a considerable amount of time and effort to the flat tax. For example, in the early 1960s, he made a strong case for a flat tax in his book *Capitalism and Freedom.*

He is far from alone. In early 1996, *The Wall Street Journal*'s editorial page carried a series of comments from a dozen well-known economists, including Friedman and several other Nobel laureates. The piece began by saying that as Steve Forbes dropped in the polls, it had become fashionable to dismiss the flat-tax idea as "nutty," and that the conventional wisdom among media pundits is that "serious" economists didn't think much of the idea. David F. Bradford, a professor of economics and public affairs at Princeton, replied that "nutty" really is the right word for today's system. Bradford, one of the most respected specialists in this field, long has advocated a gradual introduction of what he calls the "X-Tax," a plan he describes as "a close relative" of the flat tax being debated today.

The Wall Street Journal's editorial pages, headed by Robert L. Bartley, have carried extensive articles on the subject for many years. As we noted in chapter 1, it was on these pages that Hall and Rabushka introduced their plan in 1981. Bartley himself has written extensively on the subject, arguing consistently for low marginal tax rates. This concept, according to an editorial on January 30, 1996, has been "our tax lodestar."

BATTLING HEAVY ODDS

Milton Friedman and many other flat-tax proponents make it clear that they are not betting that Washington will approve a flat tax. Indeed, just the opposite now appears far more likely. After all, enactment of a pure flat tax would strip the tax-writing committees of Congress and other members involved with taxes of the enormous power they have enjoyed for generations—the power to attract huge amounts of campaign funds from business groups and people affected by their actions. Moreover, many members of Congress still believe fervently in using the tax code for social engineering, as a prod to get taxpayers to do things they believe are good for the nation or to discourage taxpayers from doing things they consider to be bad.

Add to this the strong opposition of Clinton Administration officials to the flat-tax concept. Their hostility to the Armey-Shelby plan and other pure flat-tax proposals runs very deep. The President's Council of Economic Advisers, in its annual report, blasted the idea. And the depth of the Administration's hostility was underscored in the opening words of a speech by Deputy Treasury Secretary Lawrence Summers at a Brookings Institution conference early in 1996. Since Summers was late in arriving, flat-tax guru Robert Hall filled in. After Hall sat down, Summers rose and began his speech by saying: "If I'd realized I'd be ceding time to Bob Hall, I'd have gotten here sooner."

He paused to let the laughter die down, then added: "Not that the truth has anything to fear from his words."

The ever-affable Hall smiled—weakly.

Summers then went on to deliver a withering attack on the flat tax, concluding with this point: "The flat tax is a bad idea whose time should never come." (See chapter 9 for a con-densed version of that speech.) Clinton Administration offi-cials appear to be itching to campaign against an opponent who favors the flat tax. They recall the buzz saw of criticism that former presidential candidate Jerry Brown ran into when he endorsed a flat tax.

However, do not confuse White House opposition to the flat tax with a ringing endorsement of the present system. Clinton aides make it clear that they realize the current sys-tem needs major changes. Treasury Secretary Robert Rubin, Summers, and other high-ranking Treasury officials, including Leslie B. Samuels, the assistant secretary for tax policy, em-phasize repeatedly that they are studying important ways to improve and simplify the current system. Samuels, formerly a tax lawyer from New York, often emphasizes his determination to untangle some of the code's knottier messes. One important example: the alternative minimum tax, an extraordinarily complicated set of rules designed to make many wealthy taxpayers pay at least some taxes. The AMT, as it's known, was created after a public uproar over reports that many big companies and high-income individuals weren't paying anything. Alas, the cure may have been worse than the disease. This appears to be one area the Treasury is targeting for important changes, regardless of what happens to the overall tax code.

Although Clinton aides appear to relish bashing the flat-taxers, there is widespread speculation that if President Clinton wins a second term, he will propose major tax changes, reflecting the widespread disgust with the current system. Some analysts speculate that the president might try to jump on the tax-overhaul bandwagon by endorsing a 1986-style tax bill with a flattening of tax rates, many fewer deductions, and much greater simplicity.

Chapter Eight

Back to
the Future?

In this increasingly complex world, it may be too much to expect a truly simple income-tax return. But we certainly do deserve a *simpler* system than the confusing contraption that we have created for ourselves.

Does a flat tax really have a chance? Or is the flat-tax movement doomed to follow the same ill-starred path as the Clinton Administration's health-care reform initiative?

Most political strategists we talk to instinctively reply that a pure flat tax has little or no chance of becoming law. Regardless of how appealing the flat tax may sound, it would represent an extraordinary change from the present system and may be asking our lawmakers to give up too much power at once. In the absence of a major crisis that stirs a call to arms, our political system typically moves at a glacial pace. That is especially true when one political party controls Congress and the other occupies the White House—and doubly so when the subject is as sensitive and as complex as taxes. In the wide world of taxes, change doesn't happen quickly.

But this time may be different. While talk of a pure flat tax may remain just talk, anger over the complexity of the tax code and the intrusiveness of the IRS runs so deep today that Washington may feel compelled to do something significant after all. With the House majority leader, the chairman of the House Ways and Means Committee, and many other leading political officials calling consistently for a new tax system, the chances of a major overhaul can no longer be dismissed lightly.

Purists will argue that there is nothing worth saving in our current tax code and that it should be scrapped in favor of a flat tax. Yet this does not have to be an all-or-nothing proposition. We are not required to adopt the flat-tax proposals that have been put on the table in their entirety with no changes. It is entirely possible—even plausible—that instead of adopting one or another of the various flat-tax packages, Congress might react to voter desire for a simpler tax code by moving toward a *flatter* tax system. That, of course, would fall far short of the ideal advocated by the politicians and by such flat-tax pioneers as Robert Hall and Alvin Rabushka. But it would move us toward that much-desired simplicity. More importantly, it would not require us to risk our nation's economic future on unproven theories that many mainstream economists think are fallacious, if not downright dangerous.

What, then, might the results of the debate over the flat tax be in the real world? Let's look at some of the major objectives that the flat-taxers seek and see if some compromise might be possible. We'll start with the be-all-and-end-all of the flat-tax system, the single tax rate. As even some leading flat-taxers now acknowledge privately, there is nothing sacred about a single rate. Indeed, we've already shown you that the flat tax, whether it is set at 17 percent or 19 percent, isn't really 100 percent flat anyway. The exemptions granted in the major flat-tax proposals create a progressive tax rate that hits harder as incomes rise. By abandoning the notion that there is something inherently fair about a flat tax rate that isn't really flat, we can open the discussion to the possibility of two or even more rates. If those rates were set properly, we could achieve a *flatter* tax structure than we have now while preserving some of the aspects of the tax code that many voters have found attractive.

What those rates should be and how to design a fair and simple system that won't explode the deficit are questions we will leave to professional economists, tax lawyers, and revenue estimators. But, based on our conversations with many of the nation's leading tax authorities, we have a few suggestions. First, it may be necessary to have several low rates, as in the 1986 tax act, instead of a single rate. Granted, that does not sound as simple or appealing as one rate, but it may be an answer. As *The Wall Street Journal* said in an editorial on January 30, 1996: "in principle we would have no objection to some degree of tax progressivity *so long as the highest marginal rate is reasonable.*" Looking back a decade, the editorial said a tax law with three rates topping at 28 percent "was fine by us." It added: "Without going to redistributionist extremes, there is something to be said for the ability to pay."

But in focusing on the issue of rates, let us not lose sight of the key question of *what* will be taxed and what deductions will be allowed. The most vexing deduction issue is what to do about the home mortgage interest deduction. The real-estate industry already has demonstrated its intention to fight the loss of that deduction, and it hasn't even tried yet to mobilize homeowners in a big way. Once the industry begins clamoring to save its all-time favorite deduction, the likelihood is that Congress will bow to that wish. So the question becomes how to replace that lost revenue. One way, of course, would be to raise rates. But here is another suggestion: Consider limiting how much mortgage interest may be deducted. Our current tax code typically sets a limit of $1 million on a regular mortgage; in addition, the maximum amount of home-equity debt generally is limited to $100,000 ($50,000 if you're married but filing separately). Very few homeowners have mortgages anywhere near the million-dollar mark. Thus, some tax specialists have suggested setting the cap on mortgage interest at a much lower level—say, $200,000 or $250,000. Surely, that would not deter the average citizen from achieving the American dream of home ownership. A mixture of both steps—a slight notch up in tax rates and a cap on how much interest could be deducted—might be an acceptable compromise.

A similar compromise position might be developed to deal with the question of charitable contributions. If we agree as a nation that it is desirable to promote charitable giving—and so far many people clearly have—we can fund that deduction through a slight increase in tax rates and possibly new limits on how much may be deducted in any given year. Taken together with adjustments to accommodate the home mortgage interest deduction, we might arrive at a tax code with two or three relatively low rates, while still allowing the vast majority of Americans to continue taking advantage of deductions that many people seem very reluctant to give up.

Another major goal of the flat-tax advocates is to encourage investment. They would do so by removing all taxes on interest income, dividends, and stock appreciation. We understand their point that such income is taxed twice. But as we've tried to point out, even with interest and dividend income taxed at regular income rates, and with long-term capital gains taxed at a maximum rate of 28 percent, our economy has been remarkably good at creating new jobs and even new cutting-edge industries. So why must we feel compelled to scrap that system? Why not just tweak it to achieve better performance? Even as we write this, Congress is considering a sharp cut in the capital-gains rate from its current maximum of 28 percent. Some Republican leaders want to slash the rate to a maximum of 19.8 percent. That would represent a much bigger break for investing.

Of course, at some point this fine-tuning must stop. If we retain all our current deductions, we will be back in the same boat we find ourselves in right now: a complex tax code that costs a fortune in compliance and still doesn't even come close to generating enough revenue to balance the federal budget. Someone will have to be bold enough to stand up and say "enough is enough." We freely admit that continuing to grant tax favors to one group makes it far more difficult to deny them to another. But we're dealing with political reality here. Homeowners and charities not only are powerful sources of votes in themselves, but they carry emotional appeal. Businesses, by and large, aren't regarded with much emotion; thus, simplifying the mind-boggling array of rules governing business taxes could untap lucrative new sources of revenue, allowing us to keep both individual and corporate income-tax rates relatively low. The 1986 tax overhaul suggests that politicians can stand up to special-interest groups and deny them favors if the result is something that benefits the average American citizen. And nowhere would the pickings be better than in simplifying the corporate tax code. We realize that corporations don't, in the end, pay taxes; only people do. And we certainly recognize that a higher effective tax rate on companies would be passed along in one way or another to shareholders, employees, and customers. But we keep coming back to the fact that this economy has proven itself enormously resilient through decades of taxation. We think that with moderate adjustments—adjustments that are politically achievable—the tax code can be altered to improve that performance without undertaking the immense risks inherent in a completely different tax system.

Tinkering, of course, sounds like a terrible idea to true flat-tax believers. But if, for a change, a little bit of tinkering succeeds in simplifying the system, then we will owe a significant debt to the flat-taxers each April. And that gratitude will be even greater if a simpler system with low rates encourages people to work harder, create more jobs, and improve the nation's prosperity. How much more prosperity is anyone's guess. Some tax-overhaul advocates, in a burst of enthusiasm, have argued that true tax reform could double our economic growth rate. For this, they have been sharply attacked—perhaps justifiably, since nobody we know has figured out a foolproof way to predict accurately where the economy is heading, with or without major tax-law changes. "The only function of economic forecasting is to make astrology look respectable," quips Raymond F. DeVoe, Jr., of Legg Mason Wood Walker, an investment firm in New York.

But even if our nation's economic growth rate climbs by a mere one-half of one percentage point a year, that would be a major accomplishment, says Michael Boskin, a professor of economics at Stanford University and senior fellow at the

Hoover Institution. Indeed, Boskin, who was chairman of the President's Council of Economic Advisers during the Bush Administration, says lifting our economy's growth rate by only half a percentage point each year could mark the difference between economic success and sickness over the next decade.

Thus, this may be a good time to dust off those histories of the 1986 tax act—the tax law that hardly anyone dreamed was possible and the law that seemed to die a thousand deaths until it suddenly was approved. As former House Ways and Means Chairman Dan Rostenkowski once observed, the 1986 tax act "had a lot of wakes but never a funeral."

Maybe we are heading back to the future.

Chapter Nine

Voices

As we noted in the introduction to this book, there are many people out there who are smarter than we are who have studied taxes and who have the power to influence how we tax ourselves. Their voices—both for and against a flat tax or other tax-reform measures—are worth hearing. We think you will be hearing much more from them in the future, but the following essays will introduce you to their ideas.

SENATOR BOB DOLE
SENATE MAJORITY LEADER

NOW IS THE TIME FOR A NEW TAX SYSTEM

The current tax system is broken beyond repair. It is overly complicated and grossly unfair for many taxpayers. It must be completely replaced with a new system that is fairer, flatter, and simpler—a system that will generate tremendous economic growth and allow us to eliminate the Internal Revenue Service as we know it.

The weak economic growth of the past few years is simply unacceptable. Scrapping the current tax system and replacing it with one designed to achieve economic growth will help create millions of new jobs across the country.

About a year ago, Speaker Gingrich and I established the National Commission on Economic Growth and Tax Reform, led by Jack Kemp and comprised of thirteen other commissioners from all walks of life. The commission recommended six basic principles integral to a tax system for the twenty-first century—economic growth, fairness, simplicity, neutrality, stability, and visibility.

No one could say that these important principles apply to the current tax law. Current law is tremendously unfair, and overly complex and burdensome. Taxpayers spend countless hours and billions of dollars attempting to comply with the current system—and since it is so complicated, they never really know that they computed their tax accurately—and, for that matter, neither does the IRS.

We must carefully consider the impact of any tax-reform plan on working Americans—especially those who own their own homes or hope to one day. We must ensure that in our quest to design the perfect tax system we do not actually make it harder for families to achieve the American dream of home ownership—or create a system that would reduce the value of existing homes.

It is also critical that a new tax system contain appropriate incentives for families to save for their retirement and to contribute to charity.

The central concern of any tax-reform initiative must be to provide tax relief for the millions of working families who are unnecessarily shouldering the burden of the current system.

We can never achieve our goal of greater economic growth and opportunity for all Americans by raising taxes on the middle class. In fact, we need to cut taxes on working families so they can keep more of what they earn.

In my view, the National Commission on Economic Growth and Tax Reform established the foundation for a new tax system based on economic growth and opportunity. It is now up to the American people and their congressional representatives to decide the specifics of the new system.

I have called for immediate congressional action to design a tax system that will expand the economy and create jobs. I look forward to a deliberate and thoughtful examination of various tax-reform plans and a vigorous public debate so that we design the best possible tax system for our children and grandchildren.

SENATOR RICHARD C. SHELBY OF ALABAMA

The fundamental objective of taxation is to raise enough revenue to fund the essential functions of government. It should not be used as a tool for social engineering or to manipulate the marketplace. Unfortunately, in recent years, the tax code has been used for both, and in doing so, has become the biggest, most burdensome intrusion of the federal government in people's daily lives.

In 1995, Tax Freedom Day, the day the average American taxpayer could quit working for all levels of government and start working for himself, was celebrated on May 6. This meant the average American worked two hours and forty-six minutes out of an eight-hour workday just to pay taxes.

Of course, working four months out of the year is not enough to pay taxes in the current tax code. In addition, one must take time out of his or her busy schedule, and, many times, spend money to comply with the tax code. In order to comply with the 480 tax forms and the 698 sections of the tax code, Americans are forced to pay approximately $140 billion and commit to 5.4 billion hours per year.

The Sixteenth Amendment of the Constitution gave Congress the authority to "lay and collect taxes on incomes." It did not give Congress the ability to oppress, intimidate, and harass free individuals. Neither did it intend for the tax code to be burdensome, aggravating, and inequitable. The flat tax restores the original purpose of the Sixteenth Amendment.

A flat tax would tax every dollar in the economy once and only once at the source. Since all dollars are taxed the same, government could not engineer society. The flat tax would neither encourage nor discourage economic activity, but instead let free individuals make choices based on the costs and benefits of each proposed action. This asset is known as neutrality.

A flat tax imposes one integrated flat-rate tax on individual income and business income. The individual income tax includes a generous family allowance, which in effect causes the flat tax to be progressive. The business tax is not just a replacement for the existing corporate income tax. Instead, the business tax includes all businesses, not just corporations, and interest income that is currently taxed under the personal income tax.

In addition to being simple, the flat tax is inherently fair. According to Webster's dictionary, fair is defined as "marked by impartiality and honesty; free from self-interest, prejudice, or favoritism." With its single, low, integrated rate, the flat tax fulfills Webster's definition.

A flat tax must be absolutely flat with no deductions. If we allow just one exception, such as the home mortgage interest deduction, the special-interest lobbyists will win, neutrality will be violated, and the very principle that causes so many Americans to despise politicians in Washington will be substantiated.

In addition to neutrality, an essential element of any tax reform, including the flat tax, is low marginal rates. A lower marginal rate induces much more growth than high marginal rates, which punish productivity.

Noted economists assert that the flat tax would increase growth in the economy. They only differ on how much. One established liberal Democrat economist suggests the economy would be 5.7 percent larger after five years under the flat tax. This translates into $522 billion or about $3,000 in higher income for the typical family of four.

The flat tax achieves tremendous growth by eliminating the double and triple taxation in the current tax code and by taxing every dollar in the economy once and only once. The flat tax ends the current penalties on savings and investment, thereby removing the hindrance to capital formation that ultimately leads to increased productivity. The increase in productivity will result in the growth of real income for workers. In these times of job insecurity and sluggish economic growth, the flat tax will go a long way in helping every family in America increase their wages and guarantee a bright future for their children.

REPRESENTATIVE BILL ARCHER OF TEXAS
CHAIRMAN, HOUSE WAYS AND MEANS COMMITTEE

Beyond the debate about balancing the budget and how to *spend* taxpayer money lies an equally important debate about how the government *raises* money in the first place. That debate has begun in the House Committee on Ways and Means.

I applaud the efforts of those who have drawn sharp attention to the inadequacies of the current income tax. It has become commonplace to say that the current tax code cannot be fixed and must be scrapped. However, after twenty years of efforts to reform the current tax code, I am convinced that we need to change *what* we tax, not just how we tax it.

That's why I believe we must not tinker around the edges of tax reform; we must institute a complete and fundamental overhaul of the code. I want to pull the income tax out by the roots and throw it away so that it will never grow back. In its place, I favor a tax on the consumption of goods and services.

In other words, instead of taxing people on how much money they make, we should tax people on the basis of how much they spend. Perhaps the tax could be added onto the price of purchases such as cars, haircuts, shoes, etc. Or perhaps it could be added onto the price of a product in each stage of production. Other types of consumption taxes are possible. In all cases, because the wealthy spend more, they'll pay more, but because we would no longer tax income, the new code will be simpler for everyone, so simple the IRS could be removed *entirely* from the lives of individual taxpayers.

A flat-rate income tax is an improvement over the current system, but it does not go far enough. Our nation's first income tax started as a simple tax. The law that created it was only sixteen pages long. But Uncle Sam had pulled up a chair at the payroll table, and there he sat. From the New Deal through the Great Society, the income tax grew more and more complicated—and more and more onerous.

In 1986, we attempted to make the code flatter and simpler. But its roots were left in the ground, and it began to grow again. By 1991, the tree was flourishing, with all of its complexity. In 1993, President Clinton and Congress enacted a major tax hike that further complicated the code.

Today, the tax code is 2,823 pages long—and the IRS tax regulations that implement it are more than 8,000 pages long.

Call it "Archer's maxim": any tax on income will become an increasingly complicated, graduated income tax over time. You can see this maxim at work already in the flat-rate income-tax proposals that have been made by various Republican presidential candidates. They started flat, but then deductions for home mortgage interest were added. Charitable-giving deductions will probably be next, and as history teaches us, the tree will grow again. Even a *proposed* flat-rate income tax has trouble staying flat.

On the threshold of the twenty-first century, we must not return to a nineteenth-century-style tax. Instead, we need to turn to a tax that is uniquely designed to fit the realities of today's America—one that will offer the brightest future for our people. For my part, I will use five standards to judge any proposed tax change.

FREEDOM FROM THE IRS. The new code must get the IRS completely and totally out of the lives of individual taxpayers.

Today, 120 million returns are filed each year. Whether it is on today's Form 1040 or on the "postcards" predicted by flat-rate income-tax proponents, income-tax payers will always have to send their names and earnings to the IRS. They will have to do all the necessary calculations to arrive at the correct figure. The IRS will still have to audit returns, and taxpayers will have to provide stacks of records to prove that their figures are correct.

As the first chairman of the Ways and Means Committee in memory who does his own tax return, I have pledged that I will either fix the code or suffer through it. My preference is to fix it. If we tax the consumption of goods and services instead of income, no individual would ever have to file an income tax return again.

The government's only remaining tax-collecting role would be with those who deal in goods and services—a drastically smaller number of people. The new tax system would add very little recordkeeping burden, compared to the billions of dollars a year businesses now spend on the bevies of lawyers and accountants whose only job is to comply with IRS regulations.

FAIRNESS. A consumption tax allows people to decide when and if they pay taxes—when they elect to spend. Those who spend more will pay more in taxes. Those who spend less will be taxed less. The person who pays a 10 percent tax on a Jaguar, for example, would have a higher tax bill than someone who pays a 10 percent tax on a Chevrolet. People who buy yachts would pay higher taxes than those who don't.

The new code must recognize that there are those who must spend all they earn. It must not create an undue burden on lower-income Americans. A credit, rebate, or waiver for low-income earners must be considered. Fairness is vital to successfully reforming the code.

Finally, under the consumption tax, homes would not be

taxed at all, because by definition they are not consumed items.

Reward Savings. Economists of all philosophies agree on one thing: America desperately needs to increase its savings rate. To the IRS a penny saved is a penny that ought to be taxed—more than once, if possible. This depletes the nucleus of domestic savings that is needed to provide capital for jobs in America.

A tax on spending rather than income would put a **zero** tax on savings and investments. Since income taxes will no longer be withheld from paychecks, Americans will keep their salaries to save or spend as they please. Our nation would become a sponge for savings, reducing interest rates and therefore reducing the prices of homes, cars, and other items bought on credit. The economy would grow at an unprecedented rate, providing more and higher-paying jobs.

Tax the Underground Economy. Every year, more than $100 billion in tax revenue goes uncollected because of the many people who don't report their income. Those who pay their taxes pay 10 percent to 15 percent more to make up for what is lost to the cheaters and avoiders.

Under a consumption tax, a drug dealer would pay taxes every time he bought a car, and a house painter who doesn't report his income would pay taxes every time he bought a can of paint.

To enforce an income tax, the IRS must look over the shoulder of every person with an income. This makes cheating easier and enforcement harder. The number of people who deal in goods and services is much smaller, which makes enforcement easier and less intrusive.

U.S. Competitiveness. It is my hope that in the future, conflicts between nations will not be decided on the world's battlefields, but in the world marketplace. America must position itself to be the *economic* superpower in the twenty-first century by ending taxes on income and taxing consumption instead.

The cost of paying and complying with the income tax doesn't just make U.S. products more expensive at home—it makes them less competitive overseas. A consumption tax would be removed from the price of our products as they go overseas, making them more competitive, and creating export jobs at home. In addition, foreign products would be subject to U.S. consumption tax, keeping our products competitive domestically as well. The practice is legal under international trade laws, and it is hard to overestimate the advantage this would give us in the world marketplace.

Beyond these principles for reform, many details remain to be addressed. These include determining what the tax rate would be, whether the payroll tax and the corporate tax could be eliminated, and various transitional issues as we shift from one tax system to another.

To answer these questions, in March 1996 the Ways and Means Committee began a complete and thorough review of the tax code and alternatives to it. Our effort is bipartisan and in-depth.

Only after we have heard from experts of all backgrounds—including everyday taxpayers—will we be in a position to move forward with reform. The complete abolition of the income tax is no small task. There are no panaceas, no perfect solutions. Every form of taxation will have its flaws.

Thomas Jefferson, in his second inaugural address, considered tax reform his most important achievement. He said,

"Now, it is the pleasure and pride of every American to ask, 'What farmer, what mechanic, what laborer ever sees a tax gatherer of the United States?' "

Today, that message has the same immense popular appeal it had back then. In the end, though, populist appeal is only the start. If we are going to change our system of taxation, it must be done thoughtfully and carefully.

Is it possible? It isn't only possible—the world's new realities make it crucial. And let's not forget what fueled the fire of the first American revolution. Our forebears united to end taxation without representation, to take the power to tax from a faraway place and put it in the hands of the people. Our opposition to an oppressive tax structure is what started the American project of liberty and less government.

That irresistible American impulse can carry this nation as far in the next century as it has in our past.

SENATOR PETE V. DOMENICI OF NEW MEXICO
CHAIRMAN, SENATE BUDGET COMMITTEE

A major focus of the 104th Congress has been one of utmost importance to all Americans—the future prosperity of the United States and its citizens. This focus becomes more acute as public anxiety grows over stagnant incomes and slow economic growth. One aspect of that debate centers around a plan Senator Sam Nunn and I have to abolish the current income-tax code and replace it with a progressive savings-exempt income-tax system called the "Unlimited Savings Allowance Tax" (USA Tax).

The current tax code is un-American in spirit and wrong in principle. It penalizes entrepreneurship and risk-taking, and is hostile to saving and investment. It is tilted toward consumption. It adds one third to the cost of capital, making us less competitive. It discriminates against various investment types and fares poorly in enhancing our export competitiveness. It favors debt over equity. In short, it is shortchanging our future and our children's future.

Senator Nunn and I have introduced legislation that would abolish the current income-tax code and replace it with a system that taxes income that is consumed rather than income that is earned. Income saved or invested would not be taxed until it was actually consumed. The corporate income tax would be replaced by a business cash-flow tax based on sales minus purchases and would allow investment in plant and equipment to be expensed. Our system retains current code progressivity. We envision three or four tax brackets. Preliminary work by the Congressional Budget Office suggests rates of 14, 28, and 36 percent of consumption with a zero tax rate on savings and investment.

We would install a family living allowance of $25,000 for a family of four, so families would not pay tax on the first $25,000 of consumption. The bigger the family, the larger the living allowance. Our system would include some deductions, including the home mortgage. It is a big investment.

The business tax would apply to all businesses, not just corporations, at an 11.5 percent rate on a broader tax base. To improve our export competitiveness, the business tax would be "border adjustable," meaning goods manufactured for export would not bear the burden of the USA Tax. Our system would impose a tax on imports so that goods manufactured in the United States would not be disadvantaged tax-wise over imports sold here.

Our system would also neutralize the payroll tax's adverse impact on job creation and workers by providing a credit mechanism. We would allow employees a refundable tax credit for their share of payroll taxes paid and a credit for employers for their share.

Our system is modeled to raise the same amount of revenue as our current code and to make sure that individuals and businesses continue to pay the same share of the total tax burden as under the current system.

Consumption is a better measure of the ability to pay than is income. We need a tax system that creates jobs. The American people deserve a tax code that is more fair than the current system. We want to put the American spirit of entrepreneurship back into the tax code by enacting the USA Tax. This, we believe, could allow for greater economic growth and an easing of the anxiety that now troubles too many American families.

WILLIAM G. GALE

SENIOR FELLOW IN THE ECONOMIC STUDIES PROGRAM AT THE BROOKINGS INSTITUTION IN WASHINGTON AND AUTHOR, WITH HENRY AARON OF BROOKINGS, OF *A CITIZEN'S GUIDE TO FUNDAMENTAL TAX REFORM,* TO BE PUBLISHED BY BROOKINGS IN 1996

The flat tax is an important advance in tax-policy thinking and represents a very clever and thoughtful approach to several perceived problems in the tax code and the economy. But removing the entire body of income-tax law and starting over with a whole new system is a monumental task. This is not to say that we should eschew the flat tax, only that we should approach the issue with our eyes open concerning the likely benefits, costs, and practical issues that would arise in adopting a flat tax.

POLITICAL REALITIES. The flat tax is unlikely to be adopted in its "pure" form, with no deductions. It is appropriate, therefore, to consider realistic proposals, rather than just pure flat taxes. Even the Kemp Commission allowed for the importance of deductions for mortgage interest and charitable contributions. The Commission went so far as to propose new deductions for payroll taxes and endorsed the view that existing assets need to be protected in the transition to a new tax system. Taken individually, each of these adjustments can be legitimately debated. Taken together, they seriously erode the revenue base of the flat tax.

The Treasury Department estimates that the Armey-Shelby flat tax would require a 20.8 percent tax rate to raise as much revenue as the current system. Building on that, I estimate that retaining deductions for mortgages and charity, and adding a payroll tax deduction would require a 25 percent rate. Protecting existing assets would raise the rate to 27 percent to 29 percent. Even generous allowances for economic growth due to reform reduces these rates by only one to two percentage points.

Taxes at these levels, though, may not represent reductions for most (or maybe even many) Americans and might be hard for many politicians to support. Alternatively, if the tax rate were held at 20 percent, the adjustments would raise deficits by $100 to $150 billion, unless spending cuts were enacted.

EFFICIENCY AND GROWTH. The Kemp Commission suggested that tax reform could double the U.S. growth rate for a decade. Nothing in U.S. history would suggest that this result is likely.

Recent research suggests that realistic versions of the flat tax would raise growth by only a few tenths of a percentage point over the next ten years and by very little thereafter. But even this effect may be overstated, because it rests upon a rapid increase in the saving rate that is unlikely to occur. Most U.S. saving occurs through tax-preferred vehicles, such as IRAs, 401(k) plans, Keoghs, and pensions. Funds in these accounts already receive the same tax treatment that they would under a consumption tax. And moving to a consumption tax would eliminate the early-withdrawal penalties on these accounts, which might inspire a consumption binge rather than an increase in saving. Moreover, pensions would lose their tax-advantaged status relative to other forms of saving, but may still find themselves saddled with expensive regulations, which could lead to a fall in pension coverage. Retaining mortgage-interest deductions or allowing transitional relief would reduce saving further.

SIMPLICITY. Making the tax system simpler is feasible and could reap significant gains. But the flat tax may not *stay* simple. Contrary to advocates' claims, a flat tax will not end lobbying activity. It will just start the game over at a new starting point. The same factors that led to the existing complexity—including the desire to create fair outcomes, and interest groups—would not disappear if we passed a flat tax, and would put the same pressure on the flat tax as currently exists on the income tax.

Some unintended effects will have to be dealt with as well. For example, the flat tax would essentially renegotiate every alimony agreement in the country, since alimony payments would no longer be deductible and receipts would no longer be taxable. This hardly seems like a desirable side effect of tax reform.

A new tax system would require new definitions. Even a simple statement such as "a business may deduct purchases of a business asset" requires potentially difficult legal definitions of several terms and could create expensive legal battles.

Finally, a new tax would inevitably generate unintended loopholes. For example, under the business tax, receipts from sales would be taxable, but interest income would not. In transactions with other entities (households, governments, nonprofits, or foreigners), businesses would have incentives to relabel as "interest income" as much cash inflow as possible. The other party would be indifferent. Similar possibilities occur for cash outflows. These loopholes could erode tax revenues.

Finally, moving to a new system would likely involve complicated transition rules. In short, any actual tax system will be more complex than any ideal tax system; the former is subject to the political process, must address technical details, and must raise revenue.

FAIRNESS. Proponents claim the flat tax is fair because the exemptions remove low-income households from the tax rolls and everyone pays the same rate above the exemption level. While fairness is clearly "in the eyes of the beholder," some additional points may be relevant here.

The poor would be worse off, because the flat tax eliminates the earned-income tax credit. In addition, tax reform is occurring at the same time that governments seem likely to cut real spending per beneficiary in programs that benefit low-income households. In contrast, households in the very highest income strata would see tax burdens fall. Any transitional relief for existing assets and the proposed repeal of the estate tax would further benefit wealthy households.

Many flat-tax advocates seem to be in denial mode on these issues, but the effects on the poor are a matter of simple arithmetic, and the effects on the wealthy are candidly acknowledged by Hall and Rabushka in their book. What happens to middle-class tax burdens is less clear, but would depend on whether tax reform is coupled with a tax cut, or is kept revenue-neutral.

To be clear, distributional issues should not be the only concern and may not even be a major concern of tax reform (most redistribution occurs on the spending side), but tax reform would occur against a backdrop of twenty years of increasing inequality. Taxes were not a major influence in generating this trend, but that does not imply that tax policy should exacerbate the inequality, either.

It should also be clear that there is nothing inherently fair (or unfair) about having just a single rate, but of course the flat tax has two rates—zero and, say 20 percent—not one. The case for having exactly two rates as opposed to, say, three seems difficult to make.

LOOK BEFORE YOU LEAP. There are tremendous disagreements about the effects of small policy changes that have been tried before: e.g., capital-gains tax cuts. It should not be surprising that there is a huge range of uncertainty and disagreement about large changes that have never been tried in the United States. I do not mean to suggest that fundamental tax reform is a bad idea. It is in principle a wonderful idea. But the practical difficulties, complexities, trade-offs, compromises, and risks that arise should not be taken lightly: The devil is in the details.

LAWRENCE H. SUMMERS
DEPUTY SECRETARY OF THE TREASURY

AN EVALUATION OF THE FLAT TAX

INTRODUCTION. The tax system is a tool of economic policy. To understand how it should be restructured, it is important to understand the challenges to the United States economy today.

First, there is now a bipartisan consensus on the need to balance the budget. No tax reform should compromise this essential aim.

Second, the aggregate United States economy is in very good shape. We are experiencing the first investment-led, low-inflation recovery since John Kennedy was president. Investment in equipment as a percentage of GDP has been at double-digit levels for three years in a row for the first time in thirty years. Inflation is lower than in a generation and its pernicious interaction with the tax system, which served to raise the effective rate of taxation of corporate profits and hence impede capital formation, is largely a problem of the past.

Third, the fruits of prosperity have not been shared evenly. For many years now, median wages have not risen and the real income of the least-skilled third of the population has declined by 20 percent or more. At the same time, the global economy presents an ever more attractive opportunity to a small, educated and talented minority, allowing the real income of the top 1 percent of American families to nearly double over the last decade.

These trends suggest that the current tax reform debate differs from the debates heard ten to thirty years ago. With capital costs down, investment up, inequality rising, and the middle class falling behind, the priorities of the early 1980s of providing more investment incentives, even at the expense of fairness, are not today's priorities. Today we do need to spur economic growth, but must do so in ways that ensure that its benefits are widely shared.

THE FLAT TAX. Put simply, the flat tax fails to meet present American imperatives. Start with deficit reduction. The Armey flat tax is a case in point. It is the Treasury's estimate that at the proposed 17 percent tax rate, this proposal will lose $138 billion at 1996 income levels. Making the proposal revenue-neutral so that it doesn't worsen the deficit would require imposing tax burdens at a flat rate of 20.8 percent. Bill Gale of Brookings estimates that allowing for payroll deductions, mortgage interest, and charitable deductions would add about another five percentage points. Transition relief and deductions for state and local taxes would also add about five percentage points, raising the revenue-neutral rate to about 30 percent.

Proponents suggest that these rates are not necessary because of the wondrous growth dividend a flat tax would bring about. As Yogi Berra might say, I get a sense of "deja voodoo" hearing about that sort of voodoo economics all over again.

ECONOMIC GROWTH. As for economic growth, flat-tax proponents claim it would reverse the long-term decline in private national saving by taxing consumption, not income, and thereby raising the return on savings.

Unfortunately, empirical results from past efforts to boost saving do not bear out the predictions of some standard theoretical models.

There are also ways that a flat tax could reduce saving. Current tax rules favor illiquid savings vehicles like life insurance, pensions, and IRAs, which keep money out of reach for a long time. They provide an incentive for financial institutions to sell long-term savings vehicles—something that would be lost under the flat tax.

Also, corporate saving through retained earnings is today encouraged by taxes on dividends. Retained earnings would probably fall under a flat tax, with elimination of dividend taxes. And evidence shows that these lower retained earnings would not be fully offset by higher personal saving.

FLAT-TAX HARM TO BUSINESS. The flat tax could very likely be quite burdensome for many businesses. True, it would substitute expensing for the amortization of purchases of equipment and structures. But it would also eliminate interest deductions, disallow depreciation allowances on past investments, and impose taxes on fringe-benefit payments and employer payroll taxes.

I am told that many corporate treasurers have not been pleased when they saw what their companies would pay under a flat tax. And, the non-deductibility of interest under a flat tax could severely hurt many small and medium-sized businesses or shops that are heavily mortgaged or that finance inventory with bank loans.

EXACERBATION OF BUSINESS CYCLES. I am also concerned by what a flat tax would mean for automatic stabilization of business cycles. Expensing of investment might well make corporate-tax collections highly counter-cyclical, because investment contracts sharply during recessions and rises during booms. This would increase investment during a boom and reduce it during a recession, when economic stimulus is needed the most.

All of these arguments suggest to me that the capital formation case for economic benefits of a flat tax are simply not there.

SIMPLICITY GAINS? What then about simplicity? As Herb Stein has observed, a postcard tax return is a bit obsolete when millions of taxpayers can file electronically or by pushing buttons on a telephone. A flat tax would do nothing to simplify the morass of rules regarding the definition of independent contractors or to make it easier to distinguish between personal and business use of a car or to clarify the treatment of home office deductions. Nor would tax shelters be a thing of the past. The flat tax would put far more pressure on rules that distinguish between capital and ordinary income, which some say take up one-third of the tax code.

Transition issues are another major problem. When I think of them, I am reminded of Chairman Mao's assertion that the Cultural Revolution was just a transition problem.

Think about all the IRAs in existence today. There will have to be a special provision for them thirty-five years from now when their owners retire. What is to be done with $3 trillion in future depreciation deductions for which past investments would be eligible under the present code? If these are wiped away, the playing field would be completely unfair to those who invested yesterday. But transition rules to cover these past investments would be very complex and would send present flat-tax rates even higher.

FAIRNESS. Let me turn finally to fairness. First, a flat tax would scale back the current incentive for employer-provided health insurance. Gruber and Poterba estimate that the volume of such health insurance might decline by as much as 12 percent. If only half of this decline represented a decline in the number of persons covered, this could mean nearly 10 million additional uncovered Americans.

Then there is the question of owner-occupied housing. Green, Hendershott, and Capozza estimate that the flat tax could reduce the price of housing by 38 percent and encourage substantial defaults. Even if that estimate is too high, the flat tax would clearly punish millions of Americans who made investments in reliance on the current tax code.

But, the core fairness problem stems from the income it taxes and the income it doesn't. Consider a man who inherits $10 million from the spectacularly successful investments of his father, who earns $600,000 a year on this investment, and who hires a chef who is paid $50,000 a year. Who should pay more taxes? If you think the chef should pay more, perhaps you see a fairness case for the flat tax. If not, there is a problem.

The heaviest blows would fall on the working poor and low-income families, for two reasons. These families would see their wages drop or fringe benefits reduced because of the denial of payroll-tax deductions and deductions for health insurance at the business level—they would effectively bear the burden of these taxes. Second, the Armey-Shelby flat-tax plan would eliminate entirely the earned-income tax credit (EITC).

Flat-tax advocates sometimes claim that the EITC will no longer be necessary because low-income families will be exempted from income taxes by the increased standard deductions. But these flat-tax supporters ignore the vital role of the

EITC in encouraging work and lifting the income of low-income working families.

What about the claim that the flat tax would lower marginal tax rates for many taxpayers? The average reduction in marginal tax rates is greatly exaggerated by looking only at the decline in the top marginal rate on income, which falls from 39.6 percent to 20.8 percent under a revenue-neutral version of the Armey-Shelby tax. A family of four with the estimated 1996 median income for four-person families of $48,700 would actually see their federal individual marginal tax rate increase from 15 percent to 20.8 percent. Taking account of both halves of the payroll tax and state and local income taxes (at an average state marginal rate of 5 percent), the family would see its total marginal tax rate increase from 34.6 percent to 42.7 percent under the flat tax. The increase comes about not only because of the increase in the federal marginal rate, but because of the elimination of deductions for state and local income taxes and the employer portion of the payroll tax.

Just looking at federal individual income-tax rates, the Armey-Shelby flat tax would increase marginal tax rates for 39.9 million taxpayers (28 percent), keep marginal rates the same for 41.2 million taxpayers (29 percent), and reduce marginal rates for 59.4 million taxpayers (42 percent). Marginal rates would decline or remain the same for low-income taxpayers and very high-income taxpayers. The marginal tax-rate increases would be targeted at middle-income taxpayers who are currently in the 15 percent bracket.

CONCLUSION. Let me conclude by emphasizing that the administration is committed to evaluating all proposed reforms on the criteria of fairness, efficiency, simplicity, and revenue adequacy. By that token, it would be a serious mistake to consider reforms, such as the flat tax, that would reduce revenue and interfere with our overriding national goal of reducing the deficit. Nor, given the economic developments that have unfolded over the past decade, should we be considering proposals that would shift the tax burden from upper-income to lower- and middle-income families, create serious economic disruptions, or substantially weaken federal support for important social programs and goals. Evaluated by these criteria, the flat tax has many, many problems.

AUTHORS' NOTE: Mr. Summers provided us with this paper, which is a shortened version of a speech he gave at a Brookings Institution conference on tax reform in Washington on February 16, 1996.

Appendix One

QUESTIONS AND ANSWERS

Q: The flat tax sounds too good to be true. Is it?

A: On the surface, the flat tax is remarkably simple and that accounts for a large part of its appeal. But it is simple only in that it makes it very easy for individuals and companies to figure out what tax they owe. Beyond that, it becomes amazingly complex because it raises fundamental questions about complicated social and economic issues. Many mainstream economists say that yes, it is too good to be true, that a simple tax system can't adequately deal with a society as large and complicated as ours. Flat-tax advocates, on the other hand, point to facets of their proposals that would be highly desirable, not the least of which is the emphasis on ridding the economy of the drag imposed by our current tax system. The challenge for the average voter is to understand how far-reaching a change a flat tax system would be and to realize that there are no firm answers about how individuals or the nation as a whole would fare under a flat tax.

Q: Would a flat tax be good for our country?

A: In some respects, yes, a pure and simple flat-tax system might be very beneficial. For example, a simple system would greatly reduce the vast amounts of time, energy and money we now expend trying to unravel the complexities of today's system—or paying someone else to do it for us. Estimates of the cost of compliance start as low as $75 billion and then soar into the hundreds of billions of dollars. If just a significant chunk of that money and energy could be redirected toward productive enterprise, the nation would benefit as a whole. But in other respects, the picture is much cloudier. Many analysts are sharply divided about whether it would be good for the nation to eliminate all deductions, including those for home mortgage interest, charitable donations, and state and local interest. There is also widespread disagreement about how a flat-tax system would effect the economy's overall growth rate, the savings rate, employment, and America's standing in the world economy.

Q: Does a pure flat tax really have a chance of winning approval?

A: Even the most enthusiastic flat-tax fans acknowledge it is a tough sell. For one thing, enacting a pure flat tax means asking Washington to give up the idea of trying to manipulate the economy by tinkering with the tax code, doling out benefits and subsidies here and there in an effort to promote certain types of behavior and discourage other types. Tax-code tinkering—or even threatening to tinker—has long been a great way for politicians to raise campaign funds. Thus, even many devoted fans of the flat tax aren't holding their breath waiting for it to arrive. Moreover, some people say flat-taxers face an uncomfortable dilemma. Unless we figure out a way to slash government spending, we can keep the flat rate low enough to be relatively attractive only by holding the line and saying no to many long-cherished deductions. Once we begin to give ground and make exceptions—which many people think is inevitable in view of the clout of the real-estate business, charitable institutions, and state and local governments—the rate quickly begins to climb into unattractively high territory that greatly reduces its popular appeal.

Q: That sounds pretty hopeless. Is there no hope?

A: Sure, there is some reason for hope. If the tax system continues to get more and more complicated, and if people and businesses get increasingly fed up, we could see the emergence of a flat tax, or some variation. But for that to happen would require that flat-tax advocates lay to rest the concerns of many very vocal and well-organized groups with a vested interest in keeping the current tax system. Those groups range from real-estate agents and home owners to big charities and well-financed lobbyists for big companies that enjoy large tax deductions. And don't forget that armies of tax advisers and preparers also will be lobbying for complexity. Coupled with the inherent uncertainty about what such a big change would mean for our nation's economy, that makes the job of selling a flat tax to Congress and ultimately to the voting public very difficult.

Q: How can I know if I would benefit from the flat tax?

A: Most people can't know for sure. Knowing the impact of a flat tax requires not just expertise in economics but also in mass psychology. It is very hard to know how people and businesses would react and adjust their affairs. That is the nature of our modern economy: It's simply unpredictable. So it isn't enough merely to do the simple tax calculations. There are many other factors to plug into the equation.

Q: You say most people can't know how they would be affected. Can anyone?

A: Even with all the caveats we just gave you, we can offer a few generalizations. It seems clear that very wealthy people generally would be better off. For example, anyone who stands to inherit large amounts of money obviously would benefit enormously if a flat-tax system resulted in elimination of estate and gift taxes. In some cases, that one change would overwhelm any other changes. Small-business owners have been lobbying hard for elimination of estate and gift taxes. They say the current rules all too often wind up forcing businesses and farms to be liquidated merely in order to pay taxes. Moreover, Americans generally would benefit handsomely if the flat-taxers are right that their system would truly reinvigorate the economy, leading to lower interest rates, higher corporate profits and a higher level of competitiveness for our country. Without those unproven benefits, however, there is the danger that declining house prices, higher federal budget deficits and resulting higher interest rates could hurt many taxpayers even if their direct income tax bill falls somewhat.

Q: What are some of the effects of a flat tax that might not be so obvious to the average American?

A: The average homeowner may see the price of housing decline sharply under a flat tax since one of the major inducements to own a home—the deduction for mortgage interest—would disappear under some flat-tax proposals. Also, a flat tax may affect your fringe benefits at work. Under current tax law, your company can deduct the expense of those benefits, which lowers the company's cost of providing them. Under the Hall-Rabushka flat tax, that expense would no longer be deductible. As a result, your company may choose to lower your overall compensation in some way, such as a reduction in salary or benefits.

Then there is the question of what may happen to your favorite charities if donors can no longer deduct gifts. The impact probably would be highly uneven. We have seen several studies that say many charities that depend upon very wealthy contributors for a large share of their budget would be badly hurt. But those studies also say many churches and other religious organizations might feel little or no impact. Remember that over 70 percent of all individual income-tax returns take the standard deduction, which means those taxpayers don't itemize their deductions. Naturally, gifts by these non-itemizers wouldn't be affected by elimination of the deduction. Of course, if the flat-taxers are right and flat tax helps improve the overall economy significantly, then people will have more money and overall charitable giving may increase, not decrease.

Q: Does the change to a flat tax have to be an "all-or-nothing" proposition? Can't we take some steps in that direction without committing ourselves to a wholesale overhaul of the tax system?

A: The change does not have to be all or nothing. Indeed, we think it more likely that the result of the current tax debate will be a move toward a *flatter* tax system, but not the pure flat tax that we've been discussing in this book. A flatter tax system would be one in which there are fewer and lower tax rates than in the current system. In exchange for lower rates there may be some elimination of deductions or new limits. For example, Washington might impose new limits on how much mortgage interest may be deducted. And new limits might be imposed on charitable deductions. Finally, to encourage investment—one of the central premises of the flat tax—capital-gains tax rates could be cut.

Q: Are there other ways to lower taxes?

A: Certainly. Tax rates for every American could drop substantially tomorrow if we were willing as a nation to accept substantial reductions in government spending. But it isn't clear that we're willing to do that. Our unwillingness to slash spending lies at the heart of the problems with the flat tax. Conversely, if we could agree to big spending cuts, prospects for a flat tax would brighten considerably. Some of the single rates being proposed simply don't produce sufficient revenue to keep the Washington machine running at its current speed.

Appendix Two

SPEAKING "TAXESE"

(A GUIDE TO THE ARCANE LANGUAGE OF
TAX GEEKS AND POLICY WONKS)

AMT This stands for "Alternative Minimum Tax," three dreaded words for many taxpayers. It's an extraordinarily complicated alternate system that many people and businesses must use to calculate their taxes. The AMT was born after reports that some millionaires and big corporations weren't paying any income taxes at all by using completely legal methods. The only other thing we will say about this hopelessly complicated tax is that if you may fall into its grasp, don't even think of trying to figure it out for yourself. Dump the problem on an expert.

ART Not an acronym. It's listed here merely so we can tell you an amusing story about how even the experts sometimes get a bit confused by government acronyms. Several years ago, the IRS was giving a briefing on its Art Advisory Panel, which values taxpayer donations of artworks, to a group of outside experts serving on the IRS Commissioner's Advisory Group. One puzzled man in the audience leaned over to a woman sitting next to him and whispered: "What does 'art' stand for?" The woman he asked—and the source of our story—is now the IRS Commissioner, Margaret Milner Richardson.

BACKDOOR TAX INCREASE A sneaky way to raise rates without making it really obvious. For example, in 1990, Washington approved limits on the amount of personal exemptions and itemized deductions that people are allowed to take once they reach certain income levels. That effectively pushed up the top marginal tax rate, even though the top stated rate officially remains at 39.6 percent. Don't believe the 39.6 percent rate. The people affected by it certainly don't.

CAPITAL GAINS Money you make from selling stocks, bonds, and other assets. For example, if you buy a stock for $1 and sell it for $100, you have a $99 capital gain. If you hold the investment for more than a year, it's called a long-term capital gain. If you hold it for a year or less, it's a short-term gain.

CAPITAL LOSS Money you lose when you unload an investment. Even though losses may be painful, they can also be useful. For example, under current law, you can generally offset capital gains with capital losses. If you have no gains, or if your losses exceed your gains, you may subtract as much as $3,000 of long-term capital losses each year from your ordinary income.

DEDUCTIONS Certain expenses you have incurred that you are entitled to subtract from your adjusted gross income, thus lowering your overall tax tab—unless, of course, you elect to take the "standard deduction." (More than 70 percent of all individual returns take the standard deduction.) Alas, there are some painful limits. For example, you can deduct medical expenses only to the extent that those expenses exceed 7.5 percent of your adjusted gross income.

"DIF" SCORE The IRS would rather not discuss this subject. DIF, which stands for "discriminant function," is a closely guarded secret formula used by the IRS to help figure out which returns to select for audits.

DYNAMIC SCORING This is not, as one of our colleagues once quipped, the title of a steamy new Washington sex novel. Instead, it refers to something much more arcane: a controversial method some people strongly advocate using when estimating how much more or less revenue the government would collect as a result of a proposed tax-law change. As with many Washington buzzwords, "dynamic scoring" often means different things to different people. But we will define it essentially as trying to predict how tax-law changes would affect the economy as a whole—such as the impact on gross domestic product, total employment and investment—and factoring such changes into your revenue estimate. This approach is controversial because many people think no economist on earth is smart enough to make such forecasts with enough accuracy to justify including them in revenue estimates. The opposite approach typically is known as "static analysis."

ECONOMIC REALITY That may sound like jargon for unemployment. It isn't. It's an IRS term to describe a particularly intrusive type of audit in which the agent tries to determine if a taxpayer's lifestyle and spending patterns are in line with the taxpayer's reported income. Also sometimes referred to as "lifestyle" or "financial status" audits. For example, if an agent discovers that you live in New York City in a Park Avenue co-operative apartment, drive a Lexus, belong to a Long Island country club, and have reported taxable income of only $10,000, you had better have a terrific explanation. If not, consider calling a good lawyer pronto.

EITC Stands for earned-income tax credit, which is designed to help the working poor. But tax cheats say it's so easy to take advantage of some say it really stands for: "Easy Income for Tax Cheats."

EXEMPTIONS The tax law allows personal exemptions for each taxpayer, thus cutting the amount of income subject to tax. The exact amount of the personal exemption is tied to the cost of living and thus typically rises each year. Because of exemptions and the standard deduction, many low-income people or households wind up owing no taxes at all.

FLAT TAX Any tax system that has only one official tax rate for everyone who is required to pay tax. To be more precise, it's any tax system that has only one "marginal" rate. Hong Kong comes close to having a flat tax, sort of. Even though it isn't exactly flat, it sure is simple.

FLATTER TAX An expression used by politicians who are skeptical about the flat-tax concept but want to attract flat-tax supporters' votes. What they mean precisely by this phrase is often unclear. Sometimes it means they don't like the current system but haven't yet endorsed a new one.

HOUSE WAYS AND MEANS COMMITTEE A tremendously powerful committee that has responsibility for tax legislation, among other things. Under the Constitution, all bills for raising revenue must start in the House. And in the House, tax legislation is initiated by the Committee on Ways and Means. The committee's chairman typically is one of

Washington's most important people. Critics sometimes refer to this panel as the "Committee on Ways to Be Mean."

Joint Tax Committee A little-known but highly influential Congressional committee—and not, as some comedians have suggested, a committee to tax marijuana. Its duties include serving as technical advisers to the House Ways and Means Committee and the Senate Finance Committee, as well as estimating the revenue impact of proposed tax-law changes. The committee's staff does all the hard work of drafting that incomprehensible tax-law verbiage that you later discover can change your financial life. The chairmanship of the committee typically alternates between the House and Senate. One year, it's headed by the House Ways and Means Chairman; the next year, it's the Senate Finance Chairman. The chief of staff of this committee typically is highly influential in the tax-law process. Today, it's Kenneth Kies, formerly a tax lawyer at the firm of Baker & Hostetler. The committee's full name is the Joint Committee on Taxation. It was created by the Revenue Act of 1926.

Marginal Tax Rate This tells you how much you would owe in taxes on the next dollar that you earn of taxable income.

McFlat Tax A clever title for a variant on the flat-tax idea, proposed by Indiana Representative Mark Souder. This plan preserves a deduction for mortgage (M) interest and for charitable (C) donations.

Nunn-Domenici See USA Tax Act.

Read My Lips George Bush's famous promise that he wouldn't even dream of hitting us with any new taxes. So, instead, he just raised the old ones. That's a key reason that he is now known as *former* President Bush.

Revenue Estimating The fine art of estimating the impact of proposed tax-law changes on our nation's revenues. As revenue estimators freely admit, this is hardly a pure science. To illustrate how it's done, a former Internal Revenue Service commissioner likes to tell the story of three statisticians who go duck hunting. The first one misses the duck by six inches too high. The second one misses the duck by six inches too low. "We got him!" says the third one.

Static Analysis Refers to a method used by official Washington bean counters to estimate the impact of tax-law changes—both proposed and enacted changes—on government revenue collections. It is assumed that the changes in tax laws will not affect the nation's overall economy, although changes may affect some individual economic behavior. Where those individual changes can be estimated, they are. For example, suppose Washington further cuts the deductibility of business meals. Congress's Joint Committee on Taxation could assume this would reduce the total amount spent on business meals. So "static" analysis isn't always completely static. Then there's "Dynamic Analysis," also referred to as Dynamic Scoring. That's when it *is* assumed that changes in the tax law will create change in the overall economy. Flat-tax advocates like dynamic analysis since it allows them to predict all sorts of good things for America as a result of changing to a flat tax. But they get a lot of static about that.

TCMP Ultra-intensive IRS audits in which agents require the taxpayer to justify virtually everything on the tax return. One doctor who went through the process called it "an autopsy without the benefit of dying." Some people refer to them simply as "audits from hell." TCMP stands for "Taxpayer Compliance Measurement Program." The IRS had planned about 153,000 of these audits starting in late 1995 but abruptly postponed the program because of budgetary woes. Victims are chosen more or less at random and not because the IRS suspects they did anything wrong. These audits are designed to give the IRS information about the extent of cheating that goes on, and to help it figure out where to aim its enforcement efforts in the future. That's why some people refer to these as "research audits."

TECHNICAL CORRECTION A bill to fix mistakes in previous tax laws. As one Treasury official puts it, when a lawyer makes a mistake in private practice, it's known as malpractice. But when Congress goofs, it's known as a technical correction.

USA TAX ACT Stands not for our country but for Unlimited Savings Allowance. It is a tax-overhaul plan backed by Senator Sam Nunn of Georgia and Senator Pete Domenici of New Mexico.

USER CHARGES Any of a wide variety of charges imposed by a government for services, such as passport fees and national park entrance fees. However, politicians often like to use the term "user charges" when they really mean "taxes." What's the difference between a tax and a user charge? Often, not much, as one Republican cabinet officer once acknowledged when he quipped: "I think it is simple. If it is a Democratic proposal, it is a tax. If it is Republican, it is a user fee."

VAT Stands for a "value-added tax," a system used widely outside the United States. Here is how VAT is defined by a publication of Congress's Joint Committee on Taxation: "a tax imposed and collected on the 'value added' at every stage in the production and distribution process of a good or service." In essence, as a Deloitte & Touche publication points out, the amount of "value added" is "the difference between a busi-

ness's sales revenue and purchases from other businesses."
There are several different ways to calculate the taxable base
for this. Among the enthusiasts for a VAT tax in the United
States is Representative Sam Gibbons, the ranking Democrat
on the House Ways and Means Committee.

STEVE FORBES'S FLAT-TAX FORM

1. Wages & salary   1 _____

2. Taxpayer exemptions

    (a) $26,000 for married filing jointly

    (b) $13,000 for single

    (c) $17,000 for single head of household   2 _____

3. Number of dependents, not including spouse   3 _____

4. Deductions for dependents

    (line 3 multiplied by $5,000)   4 _____

5. Total deduction (line 2 plus line 4)   5 _____

6. Taxable income (subtract line 5 from line 1)   6 _____

7. Tax (17% of line 6)   7 _____

ARMEY-SHELBY FLAT-TAX FORM
—————————— 1998 ——————————

1. Wages, salary and pensions   1 _____

2. Personal allowance

    (a) $22,700 for married filing jointly

    (b) $11,350 for single

    (c) $14,850 for single head of household   2 _____

3. Number of dependents, not including spouse   3 _____

4. Personal allowances for dependents

    (line 3 multiplied by $5,300)   4 _____

5. Total personal allowances (line 2 plus line 4)   5 _____

6. Taxable wages

    (line 1 less line 5, if positive, otherwise zero)   6 _____

7. Tax (17% of line 6)   7 _____

8. Tax already paid   8 _____

9. Tax due (line 7 less line 8, if positive)   9 _____

10. Refund due (line 8 less line 7, if positive)   10 _____